insight text guide

Victoria Bladen

Much Ado About Nothing

William Shakespeare

First published in 2019, reprinted in 2020 (twice), 2021.

Insight Publications Pty Ltd
3/350 Charman Road
Cheltenham VIC 3192
Australia
Tel: +61 3 8571 4950
Fax: +61 3 8571 0257
Email: books@insightpublications.com.au

www.insightpublications.com.au

A catalogue record for this book is available from the National Library of Australia

William Shakespeare's Much Ado About Nothing / Victoria Bladen

ISBNs:
9781925778427 (print)
9781925778434 (digital)
9781925778441 (bundle: print + digital)

Cover design by Gisela Beer, based on a concept by The Modern Art Production Group

Printed by Markono Print Media Pte Ltd

This book is dedicated to the memory of Emily John, who loved Shakespeare.

contents

CHARACTER MAP

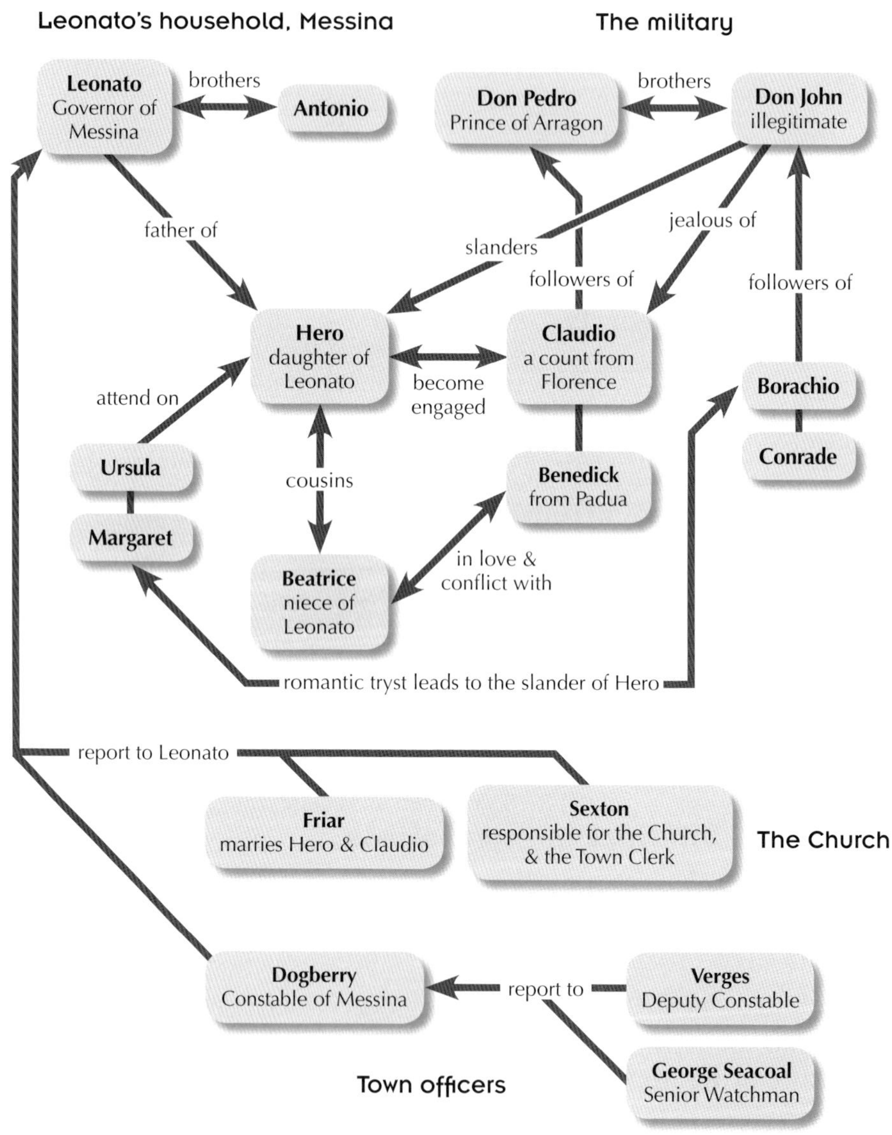

OVERVIEW

William Shakespeare (1564–1616) is one of the most renowned figures of the English literary Renaissance (also referred to as the 'early modern period'). His dramatic and poetic works, written during an intensely productive period from the late sixteenth to the early seventeenth century, have proved capable of enduring well beyond his own time and place. Translated into many languages and adapted for film, television, ballet, opera and graphic novels, Shakespeare's work has evolved into a cultural phenomenon, meaningful and compelling to audiences of different periods and cultures.

Much Ado About Nothing is one of Shakespeare's most popular comedies, and it presents us with two sets of lovers who have to resolve their conflicts and misunderstandings. Remember that *Much Ado About Nothing* is a *play*, created to be experienced as a performance on stage, even though it is often first encountered as a written text or as a film. If you are able to see the play performed, you will gain a deeper understanding of its shape and characters, how the dramatic action unfolds and the effect of Shakespeare's language. Film adaptations will also help you to understand the play, particularly if you are able to view different versions; you may even be able to see a filmed stage production. However, remember that watching a film should not be a substitute for a close reading of the text itself.

About the author

Shakespeare was born in 1564, when Elizabeth I was on the throne, and died in 1616, when James I was king. Born into a middle-class family in Stratford-upon-Avon, in Warwickshire, William was the son of John Shakespeare, a glove-maker and landowner, and his wife Mary (whose maiden name was Arden), a gentleman's daughter. Shakespeare received an education from the King's New School in Stratford, but never attended university. As a young man, he fell in love with Anne Hathaway, and they were married in 1582 after Anne became pregnant; the child, Susanna, was born six months after the wedding. Twins, Hamnet and Judith, were born in 1585; Hamnet died as a child. Subsequently, the marriage appears to have broken down.

In the late 1580s, Shakespeare moved to London and began his career as a playwright. He joined a theatre company called The Lord Chamberlain's Men (also briefly known as Lord Hunsdon's Men), under the patronage of the Lord Chamberlain. The ensemble produced plays that were performed at a venue called the Theatre. He acted in and wrote plays for this company, and also shared in the profits. When the lease over the land on which the Theatre was built expired in 1597, and a dispute arose with the landlord, Shakespeare and his colleagues dismantled the wooden building, took it across the river and reassembled it. This theatre, renamed the Globe, opened in 1599. In London today, Shakespeare's plays are performed year-round in a close replica of the Globe, near the original site. There is also an indoor theatre, the Sam Wanamaker Playhouse, which is modelled on indoor theatres from Shakespeare's period.

When James I came to the throne in 1603, he became patron of the theatre company of which Shakespeare was part owner; the company was therefore renamed the King's Men. The King recognised the huge potential of the theatre to reach many people; the theatre can perhaps be thought of as the early-seventeenth-century equivalent of television or the internet. James wanted his reign to be associated with that 'media' power, despite the fact that in many of Shakespeare's works there is strong criticism of authority figures.

Synopsis

Much Ado About Nothing is a play about the conflict between men and women, even when they are in love, and perhaps precisely because they are in love. It is also about the dangers of misreading, and mistaking appearances for reality. The play is set in Messina, Sicily, an island south of the Italian mainland, where Leonato, the Governor of Messina, welcomes Don Pedro, the Prince of Arragon, from the northeast of Spain. Don Pedro's entourage includes Benedick and Claudio, who have fought with Don Pedro in a recent military campaign. Claudio falls in love with Hero, Leonato's daughter, while Benedick claims to detest Beatrice, niece of Leonato. Both sets of lovers will undergo a traumatic courtship journey before all is eventually resolved with a comic (happy) ending.

In the first act, Don Pedro and his companions arrive in Messina after fighting in local military conflict, and seek hospitality from Leonato, Messina's governor. Leonato proposes a masked ball, which will take place in Act 2. We are introduced to the witty and sparring Beatrice and Benedick, and learn that they have had some kind of courtship previously that has left them both bitter. Don Pedro proposes that he woo Hero on Claudio's behalf at the masked ball. Meanwhile Don John, Don Pedro's surly and melancholy brother, hears of the wooing plan, and proposes to make use of it to create mischief, as he is resentful of his brother Don Pedro, and jealous of Claudio's recent advancement.

In the second act, the masked ball takes place, at which Don Pedro woos Hero for Claudio, and Beatrice has the opportunity to insult Benedick. The next day, Don John expresses his displeasure at the news of Claudio and Hero's engagement. Don John's follower Borachio proposes a plan to stage the appearance of a liaison between himself and Hero, exploiting Borachio's relationship with Hero's lady-in-waiting Margaret. Meanwhile Benedick is tricked by his companions when he overhears them talk of Beatrice's supposed love for him. Benedick is convinced by the trick and resolves to marry Beatrice.

The tone of the third act shifts between darker and lighter moods. Beatrice is tricked by her companions into believing Benedick is in love with her and resolves to return his love. Events take a more sinister turn when Don John tells Claudio that Hero has been unfaithful with Borachio, thus threatening the wedding. We are introduced to the incomprehensible constable Dogberry and his companions who, despite their incompetence, manage to uncover the plot against Hero and Claudio, and arrest Borachio and Conrade. Hero and her attendants prepare for the wedding. Dogberry attempts to tell Leonato what they have discovered, but miscommunications hamper the process. Leonato, none the wiser, leaves Dogberry in charge of the examination of Borachio and Conrade and hurries off to prepare for the wedding.

Act 4 presents the dramatic climax of the play when, instead of going through with the wedding, Claudio uses the gathering to publicly slander Hero, whereupon she faints as if dead. Leonato, believing the accusations instead of trusting the character of his daughter, bemoans the loss of her reputation, and wishes her dead rather than unchaste. Once Claudio and Don Pedro exit, the Friar attempts to calm the family by suggesting that they pretend that Hero has in fact died, in the hope of a positive outcome. The crisis brings Benedick and Beatrice together; however, Beatrice demands that Benedick kill Claudio in revenge, testing Benedick's loyalties. Meanwhile, Dogberry bungles through an examination of Don John's men.

In the final act, Leonato expresses his grief to his brother Antonio, and Claudio seems little moved by Hero's reported death until the slander plot is revealed, thanks to Dogberry and Verges. Claudio, now remorseful and grieving, agrees to marry Leonato's 'niece' (Hero in disguise) as recompense. Claudio attends Hero's 'tomb', accompanied by Don Pedro, to read an epitaph. At the wedding, Hero is veiled so Claudio only discovers her identity after he is married, at which point they are reconciled. Benedick and Beatrice are proved to be in love by their sonnets written to each other. The play ends on a joyful note with Leonato proposing a dance and news arriving that Don John has been captured.

Character summaries

Don Pedro: Prince of Arragon, Spain; he was recently involved in a military campaign.

Don John: the illegitimate half-brother of Don Pedro; he instigates the slander against Hero.

Benedick: from Padua; he accompanies Don Pedro and engages in a war of wits with Beatrice.

Claudio: a count from Florence; he accompanies Don Pedro and falls in love with Hero.

Borachio: a follower of Don John; his name means a drunkard.

Conrade: another follower of Don John.

Leonato: Governor of Messina, and Hero's father.

Antonio: Leonato's brother.

Hero: the daughter of Leonato; becomes engaged to Claudio. She is the victim of Don John's slander plot.

Beatrice: Leonato's niece; she engages in a war of wits with Benedick.

Margaret and Ursula: members of Leonato's household, and ladies-in-waiting to Hero.

Balthasar: a singer; follower of Don Pedro.

Friar Francis: officiates at the wedding of Claudio and Hero; advises Leonato.

Sexton: responsible for the Church; as Town Clerk, he presides over Dogberry's examination of Borachio and Conrade.

Dogberry: Constable of Messina.

Verges: Deputy Constable.

George Seacoal: Senior Watchman.

First Watchman and Second Watchman: report to Dogberry.

BACKGROUND & CONTEXT

Much Ado About Nothing is set in Messina, Sicily. At this time, Sicily was governed by Spain. Consequently, Leonato is obliged to provide hospitality and entertainment to Don Pedro, Prince of Arragon, and his soldiers, who have been involved in a military campaign nearby.

Note that throughout this guide, references to lines in the play use numbers that refer to the act, scene and line. So, for example, a reference 2.4.10 means Act 2 Scene 4, line 10. For conciseness, the play's title is frequently shortened to *Much Ado*.

The position of women

In the early modern period, women were perceived as socially and intellectually inferior to men. This belief originated with the Bible and the construction of Eve as secondary to and created from Adam. It was assumed women belonged in the home and they were generally excluded from matters of state and warfare. Women were also expected to be chaste, obedient and silent.

Women were often treated as beautiful possessions, rather than active individuals with their own thoughts and rights. Daughters were thought of, and considered by the law, as the property of their fathers or husbands. This ideology is reflected in the plays of the period, including Shakespeare's, although characters like Beatrice challenge and resist this construction of women.

Cuckoldry

Related to the construction of women as unreliable was male anxiety over wives being unfaithful. There was no DNA testing at this time, thus no way of determining who a child's biological father was. Fathers wanted to be certain their children were their own because property passed from a man to his eldest son upon a father's death. Anxiety over infidelity is a common topic of jokes and teasing across Shakespeare's work, including in *Much Ado*.

The word 'cuckold' derives from the Middle English adaptation of an old French word for cuckoo. The cuckoo lays its eggs in the nests of other birds, who then unknowingly raise its chicks, and so it became a symbol of infidelity. For a husband to be 'cuckolded' or a 'cuckold' meant that another man had slept with his wife. The common symbol for being a cuckold was horns on the head; the origin of this may be that a horned beast cannot see his own horns. So in a Shakespearean play, when you encounter a reference to horns, it is most likely a joke about cuckoldry. For example, Benedick says that if he ever submits to marriage, his companions should 'pluck off the bull's horns, and set them in my forehead' (1.1.196), meaning they should assume that his wife is cheating on him.

Class

Shakespeare's society was hierarchical and class differences between the various characters are significant. A key distinction in early modern society was between the lower classes (such as the Watchmen) who laboured for their income, and 'gentlemen' and 'gentlewomen' ('the gentry', such as Beatrice, Hero, Leonato and Benedick), who did not have to work for a living because they had sufficient income from property and inherited sums. Margaret and Ursula, although they attend on Hero, are nevertheless gentlewomen, as women at court usually were. Similarly, Borachio and Conrade, who attend on Don John, are likely to be gentlemen. Dogberry and Verges, as the constable and deputy constable, may be gentlemen, as it was usually necessary to have some social standing to be appointed as a town official.

There were further distinctions among the upper class between the mere gentry and the aristocrats, who inherited their titles and large landed estates. The aristocracy was itself ranked between various levels from the monarch at the top, followed by dukes and ending with barons, the lowest inherited title. Don Pedro is a Spanish prince, so he is ranked at the top of the social hierarchy. Don John, although he is Don Pedro's brother, is illegitimate, so he doesn't share the same high ranking as Don Pedro, although Don John is still a gentleman. Claudio is a count, which is a high-ranking aristocrat, although not as high as a duke. Leonato and his brother Antonio are gentlemen and Leonato also has political status as the governor.

With the shift in the early modern period from a feudal system (based on an exchange of service and protection) towards a more proto-capitalist one (based on the exchange of money for labour or goods), the merchant class emerged, creating new forms of social mobility. As an example, Shakespeare's father John, who was a glove-maker, held various official positions in Stratford. During Shakespeare's lifetime, he applied for (and was granted) a family coat of arms in order to be recognised as a gentleman.

Humours

The human body was thought to be composed of four humours: blood, choler, melancholy and phlegm. Different characteristics were associated with each of these substances, and their proportions in a person dictated their personality. Imbalances in the humours were believed to cause adverse health effects and particular behaviours. Don John is surly and unsociable; he suffers from excess melancholy in his constitution (1.3.1–4). In the first scene, Beatrice refers to her 'cold blood', claiming to be like Benedick: 'I am of your humour' (1.1.96–7). Another reference to the humours comes in 2.1 when Leonato observes that 'there's little of the melancholy element' in Beatrice (2.1.259), meaning that she has a higher proportion of the 'blood' element, associated with an optimistic, happy outlook.

Mythology and legends

The English Renaissance period (from the late 1400s to 1660) was one of intense literary production that included a revival of interest in classical Greek and Roman literature. English Renaissance literature commonly refers to classical mythology – tales of gods and goddesses – and you will notice this in Shakespeare's plays. Such references can add grandeur to a character. Alternatively, they may be used for parody and comic effect, as when Beatrice refers to Benedick as challenging Cupid to a competition (suggesting Benedick's vanity and his pride in being attractive to women, 1.1.29–31); or when Benedick says 'Cupid is a good hare-finder, and Vulcan a rare carpenter' (1.1.136–7), relying on the audience's knowledge of common mythological figures. Also, Don Pedro describes the challenge of bringing Benedick and Beatrice together as 'one of Hercules' labours' (2.1.275); Hercules took on twelve superhuman feats.

In 2.1, when Benedick is trying to avoid seeing Beatrice, and asks Don Pedro to send him on an errand 'to the world's end' (2.1.199), Benedick makes several legendary allusions. The 'Antipodes' (2.1.200) refers to the lands in the southern hemisphere, which were unknown to most Europeans, even though travel and exploration were expanding during Shakespeare's lifetime. On medieval and early modern maps, various exotic races were located at the edge of the known world; the 'Pygmies' (2.1.204) were one such race. 'Prester John' (2.1.202) was a legendary figure who was thought to govern a Christian kingdom somewhere in Africa. The 'Great Cham' (2.1.203) was a Mongol emperor. These references are intended to conjure exotic and faraway places, and to convey Benedick's desire to get as far away from Beatrice as possible.

Love and sonnets

In the late sixteenth century there was a sonnet craze in England. Most writers tried their hand at this poetic form, including Shakespeare, who wrote 154 sonnets. A sonnet is a fourteen-line poem with particular rhyming patterns. The European tradition of sonnets began with the fourteenth-century Italian writer Petrarch. The Petrarchan sonnet consisted of an octave (an eight-line stanza), a sestet (a six-line stanza), and a rhyming pattern: *abbacddc efgefg*. What became known as the 'Shakespearean sonnet' has three quatrains (stanzas with four lines) and a couplet (two lines), usually with a rhyming pattern of: *abab cdcd efef gg*.

From the time of Petrarch, the sonnet form was associated with love. Sonnets were written to a beloved and might praise her or him, expressing love and longing. In several of Shakespeare's plays, including *Much Ado About Nothing*, writing sonnets is linked with characters in love.

The plague

In the first scene of the play, Beatrice makes a joke about Benedick being like the 'pestilence' (1.1.63) or plague. Plague was a serious disease in Shakespeare's time. It spread across Europe in waves and there was no cure. Carried by fleas on rats, the cause of the disease was not understood. Shakespeare was lucky to survive into adulthood as, at the time of his birth, many people in Stratford died of the plague. Beatrice uses the reference to suggest that Benedick will cause his companions misery.

Publication history

There are no surviving draft manuscripts, notes or diaries left by Shakespeare, so scholars have to piece together other evidence to determine approximately when a play was written. Even then, there is often debate about the date of Shakespeare's plays. Plays were often revised during production and published in different versions, so the idea of a definitive version of a Shakespeare play is problematic. *Much Ado About Nothing* is believed to have been written in 1598 and first performed in the same year. There is one theory that *Much Ado* is a sequel to the earlier play *Love's Labour's Lost* and is in fact the play that was originally titled *Love's Labour's Won*, a 'lost play' of Shakespeare's. In *Love's Labour's Lost*, the sparring lovers Biron and Rosaline resemble Beatrice and Benedick in several aspects. Critics are divided on the connection between the two plays and whether *Much Ado* is the lost play, but one production went as far as to rename *Much Ado* as *Love's Labour's Won*. After studying *Much Ado*, you may like to read *Love's Labour's Lost* and make up your own mind about whether the two plays might be connected.

One edition of *Much Ado About Nothing* (the Quarto edition) was published in 1600, during Shakespeare's lifetime; the play was published again in 1623, in the First Folio (a collection of nearly all of Shakespeare's plays). The Quarto text is interesting because it bears marks of being very close to Shakespeare's original draft. For example, in one place the speeches for the character of Dogberry are labelled 'Kemp', which refers to Will Kemp, a comic actor in Shakespeare's company. Clearly Shakespeare was thinking about the actor for whom he was writing the role.

You might notice that different editions of the play use alternative spellings for Benedick. In this text guide, we follow the Cambridge School Shakespeare text in using 'Benedick'; however, in the First Folio edition, the editors used 'Benedict'.

GENRE, STRUCTURE & LANGUAGE

Genre

In the 1623 First Folio, the editors divided the plays into three genres: comedies, tragedies and histories. *Much Ado* is a comedy: that is, it resolves the plots with a happy ending. Although the play is comic in genre, it does have a dark vein. The Hero plot has the potential to turn tragic (as in *Othello*, one of Shakespeare's tragedies, in which the plot of a falsely accused woman ends with multiple deaths). Hero appears to die, like Hermione in *The Winter's Tale* (another Shakespearean play that uses the motif of the falsely accused woman). Like Hermione, who appears to be a statue that is brought to life, Hero seems to come back to life once her accuser has repented of his slander.

Shakespeare's later comedies, such as *Measure for Measure* and *All's Well That Ends Well*, have been classified as problem comedies because, although there is a reconciliation at the end, some elements remain unsettling or unresolved. Although *Much Ado* is not a problem comedy, there are some troubling aspects. Does Claudio deserve Hero in the end, and will he prove a good husband to her? Also, if Beatrice and Benedick have been brought together on false pretences, how genuine are their feelings?

Although there is no specific source for the Beatrice and Benedick plot, the Claudio and Hero plot has Italian precedents in Ludovico Ariosto's *Orlando Furioso* (1516) and Matteo Bandello's *Novelle* (1554), plays that Shakespeare may have been aware of. Baldassare Castiglione's *The Book of the Courtier* (1528) provided advice for courtiers on how to behave and is relevant to Shakespeare's depiction of witty repartee between the courtiers in *Much Ado*. The conversations in the play are examples of courtly behaviour; they are both performances and demonstrations of skill.

Structure

The play interweaves two main threads that develop the narrative of two sets of lovers: Beatrice and Benedick; and Claudio and Hero. All the scenes take place in Messina over a few days, so the action is unified in time and place; there are no large leaps in time. The first act juxtaposes the talkative, sparring lovers Benedick and Beatrice with Claudio and Hero, who are less skilled in communication. It also brings together the two key groups of characters: the military leader Don Pedro and his soldiers; and Leonato, the governor of Messina, and his household. Don John's bitter nature signals trouble ahead.

The masked ball at the beginning of Act 2 enables the characters to interact in a less guarded way, and to reveal emotions that will drive the plot. There are dialogues between different pairs of characters, structured to give the audience a feeling of moving through the ball and eavesdropping on various conversations.

Act 3 shifts between different moods with scenes that build the sinister slander plot, and those with more lighthearted elements. After 3.2, once Don John has poured his poison in the ears of Claudio and Don Pedro, the atmosphere becomes darker. However, in 3.3 we shift focus to the lower-class characters, who bring a humorous element and whose bungling will expose the plotters. There are parallels between what is happening among the upper-class and lower-class circles. The slander of Dogberry, who is called an 'ass' by Conrade (4.2.60), echoes and parodies that of Hero; the serious consequences at the high end contrast with humour at the low end.

The crisis of Act 4 contains the potential for tragedy with Hero's seeming death. The effects of this ripple out and form a catalyst for Benedick and Beatrice's union, and Benedick's shift in loyalty from his companions to Beatrice. The final act contains a second dramatic climax, with the second wedding ceremony and the revelation of the true Hero. In the denouement (the tying up of ends), Benedick and Beatrice are brought together by their companions producing the lovers' sonnets.

Language

Shakespeare was a gifted wordsmith, inventing many new words and playing on the multiple meanings of a word. Shifts in a conversation often hinge on wordplay, where a word is used in one sense by one character, then in a different sense by another.

You will also notice Shakespeare's constant use of metaphors to describe people, emotions and events. This technique, common in Renaissance literature, adds depth and complexity to the language of the play through the mental images that the words evoke. Language is also important in communicating the respect or disrespect that various characters have for each other. They convey loyalty, love and friendship bonds through language.

In *Much Ado About Nothing*, language is important for displaying the skills of the courtiers, and showing off their education, a mark of their social status. They play with language to create puns and patterns, creating links and associations. They also use rhetorical techniques for emphasis. For example, Benedick uses anaphora (the repetition of a word at the beginning of successive phrases or sentences) when he says 'too low for a high praise, too brown for a fair praise, and too little for a great praise' (1.1.126–7).

Shakespeare's playing with language is even apparent in the play's title. In Shakespeare's time, the word 'nothing' sounded similar to 'noting' (observing), and these ideas are closely linked. Much ado – a fuss and uproar – is created over an allegation that has no foundation; it is nothing. It all comes about by 'noting', or observing; some of this observing is misleading, such as what Claudio *thinks* he sees; while other observing, such as that by the incompetent Dogberry and his men, will lead to discovering the deception. 'Nothing', evoking the idea of a circular zero, was also a bawdy term for the vagina, which is relevant given that the theme of the play is centred on the allegation of a woman's infidelity.

Indeed, Shakespeare often uses bawdy language, slang terms for bodily parts and sexual functions. For example, when Benedick says 'and a case to put it into' (1.1.135), he is making a sexual joke as 'case' was a word for female genitalia. When Leonato in 2.1 says 'half Signor Benedick's tongue in Count John's mouth' (2.1.9), although it is about the characters' loquacity (talking a lot), the audience would no doubt pick up the bawdy homoerotic innuendo.

Comedy is an important aspect of the language in *Much Ado*, particularly in the speeches of the warring Beatrice and Benedick. Much of the humour arises from the various insults that they inflict on each other. Also note how comic elements are created through Dogberry's speech and his misunderstanding of the words he chooses. His malapropisms (words that sound similar to the ones he intends but that have a different meaning) cause bewilderment and confusion, creating comic situations.

As you are reading the play, note where the language shifts between verse and prose. Prose writing has no regular pattern to the stressed and unstressed syllables of words. It is characterised in print by lines running to the edge of the margin, and is the form we use in ordinary writing and speech. Verse, however, has patterns of stressed and unstressed syllables. In Shakespeare's work the verse lines are usually in iambic pentameter – there are generally five 'beats' or stresses to the line with unstressed syllables in between (ten syllables in total), creating a 'da DUM' rhythm. There are variations on this, particularly at the beginnings or endings of lines, but this is the overall pattern. The rhythm of verse creates a sense of order and a heightened focus on the words. In many of Shakespeare's plays, the upper-class characters speak mostly in verse, while the lower-class characters speak in prose. In *Much Ado*, the play begins in prose, but shifts into verse at certain moments, such as when the topic of love is brought up in Act 1. Changes between prose and verse can be used to create particular effects, for example to introduce the idea of the heightened state of love, as well as the common link between love and poetry.

SCENE-BY-SCENE ANALYSIS

Act 1

1.1 Summary: *Don Pedro and his company arrive in Messina where they are welcomed by Leonato. Claudio falls in love with Hero. Benedick and Beatrice meet again and engage in a war of insults.*

We hear of recent military action in which Claudio, from Don Pedro's company, was honoured; ironically, it seems that he was braver in battle than he will be in wooing. Beatrice ridicules Benedick, another soldier in Don Pedro's company, although the fact that she asks after him suggests she is secretly concerned as to whether he survived. Leonato refers to the 'merry war' between Beatrice and Benedick (1.1.45–6). This sets up the link between love and war. Beatrice takes control of the conversation and imagines Benedick as a type of plague. Leonato is expected to provide hospitality; although Don Pedro refers to Leonato having 'invited' his company (1.1.109), Leonato has little choice. Interestingly, the references to 'trouble' (1.1.71; 1.1.73) foreshadow the trouble the company will create for Leonato and his family.

One of the humorous points in the scene occurs when Beatrice says, 'I wonder that you will still be talking, Signor Benedick, nobody marks you' (1.1.86–7); it wounds Benedick's pride, but also shows that Beatrice is listening to him. When Benedick retreats from their verbal skirmish, Beatrice says 'I know you of old' (1.1.107). This suggests that she and Benedick have had some kind of past relationship.

When Claudio confesses to Benedick his attraction to Hero, note how they slip into the language of property. Benedick asks if Claudio would like to 'buy her' and Claudio replies 'Can the world buy such a jewel?' (1.1.133–4). Claudio's line 'In mine eye, she is the sweetest lady that ever I looked on' (1.1.139) introduces the theme of sight. But Benedick is sceptical of Claudio's feelings and he outlines various reasons why it would be better to remain a bachelor, such as the necessary restraint on a man that marriage entails, and the risk of cuckoldry.

Note Benedick's ominous reference to an English version of the tale of Bluebeard (1.1.160–1), a story of a man who killed his wives. This is another example of foreshadowing, since Claudio's slander of Hero will appear to kill her.

Claudio is shown to be of a suspicious mind; when Don Pedro states his opinion that Hero is worthy, Claudio assumes that Don Pedro is only saying this to trick him (1.1.165). When Benedick claims that he will not do women wrong by mistrusting them (1.1.180–1) – in other words, he won't marry them in the first place – this again foreshadows what Claudio will do wrong, mistrusting Hero.

Claudio asks Don Pedro whether Leonato has a son because he wants to find out whether Hero will inherit any money. Claudio asks Don Pedro to speak on his behalf to Hero and her father; however, Don Pedro goes further than this and proposes to pretend to be Claudio at the masked ball and woo Hero on Claudio's behalf. We don't know what Claudio's thoughts on this are because he isn't given a speech, but directors and actors would need to decide how Claudio feels. He may well feel apprehensive, particularly given the latent violence in the words that Don Pedro uses. The language is that of soldiering: 'take her hearing prisoner with the force / And strong encounter of my amorous tale' (1.1.250–1).

Note the various literary devices used in this scene: *chiasmus*, where a phrase is repeated in reverse: 'How much better is it to weep at joy, than to joy at weeping' (1.1.21–2); *simile*: 'He will hang upon him like a disease' (1.1.62); and *anaphora* (the repetition of phrases): 'too low … too brown … too little' (1.1.126–7).

Key point

Most of the first scene is written in prose; however, after Benedick exits at 1.1.215, leaving Claudio and Don Pedro, the form of the dramatic dialogue changes to poetry, specifically blank verse (without rhyme) in iambic pentameter. The reason for this shift is that the subject turns to love, a subject that was associated with poetry in the English Renaissance. Poetry is concentrated, elevated language, thought fitting for the emotions of love. This link between love and poetry will reappear later in the play.

1.2 Summary: *Antonio passes on misheard information to his brother Leonato.*

Antonio, Leonato's brother, passes on information that his servant overheard when Don Pedro and Claudio were talking in Antonio's orchard. The overhearing is an example of the play's theme of surveillance and reading or misreading information. The servant has misunderstood, mistakenly believing that the Prince, rather than Claudio, was confessing his love for Hero. This foreshadows Claudio's subsequent misreading. Note, however, that Leonato is less inclined to jump to conclusions; he will only think of it 'as a dream' (1.2.16) until he has better evidence. Leonato thus provides a model of behaviour that Claudio would do well to follow.

1.3 Summary: *Borachio tells Don John of the engagement news and Don John considers how he can use it to create mischief by spiting his brother Don Pedro and interfering with Claudio's happiness.*

Don John's excessive sadness arises from an excess of melancholy in his constitution, according to early modern humoral theories. His reference to Conrade being born under the sign of Saturn also reflects the period's common beliefs about the influence of the stars.

We find out that there has been recent conflict between Don John and his brother Don Pedro, but that Don Pedro forgave him (1.3.16). Then the characters use a series of natural and agricultural metaphors. Conrade refers to Don John taking 'true root' (1.3.17) – establishing himself and his true nature – and advises him to 'frame the season for your own harvest' (1.3.18–19), or to orchestrate events to produce the outcomes that he wants. Don John picks up this vein of imagery, claiming he would rather be a 'canker in a hedge' (1.3.20) – a wild rose. This touches on his illegitimacy; he is a 'wild' flower, growing outside of marriage and society's approval, rather than one within a garden, a legitimate plant/offspring.

Borachio brings news of the intended wooing of Hero by Don Pedro on Claudio's behalf. He too has been overhearing but, unlike Antonio's servant, Borachio has heard correctly. Don John expresses his jealousy of and resentment towards Claudio, since he perceives Claudio as benefitting from Don John's fall from favour, even though the two events are independent. (We know from the first scene that Claudio has been honoured because of his actions in the recent military conflict.) Don John considers how he can put this information to ill use.

Key vocabulary

hot January (1.1.69): an oxymoron since January in the northern hemisphere is cold.

jade's trick (1.1.107): trick of an old horse; stopping/retreating.

recheat winded in my forehead, or hang my bugle in an invisible baldric (1.1.179–80): references to cuckoldry; recheat was a hunting call on a horn; a baldric was a belt to hold the horn.

hang me in a bottle like a cat, and shoot at me (1.1.191): a cruel Elizabethan pastime was to put cats in hanging baskets and aim at them with bow and arrow.

thick-pleached (1.2.8): enclosed by trees with boughs intertwining.

take the present time by the top (1.2.11–12): opportunity was often personified as a woman who was bald except for a forelock of hair, which one had to quickly grasp, in order to take advantage of opportunity.

sad conference (1.3.43–4): serious discussion.

start-up (1.3.48): young and rising in social status.

Q How well does Claudio know Hero before he decides to marry her, and what risks does this create?

Q Analyse some of the relationships between pairs of characters, such as Beatrice and Benedick; and Don Pedro and Leonato. How will these shift throughout the play?

Act 2

2.1 Summary: *Leonato and his company enter the masked ball. Don Pedro woos Hero for Claudio and Beatrice has the opportunity to insult Benedick.*

At the masked ball, Beatrice comments on the fact that an ideal man would be one who talks more than the taciturn Don John but less than the loquacious Benedick. This shows that Benedick remains on Beatrice's mind, even though she appears to be criticising him.

When Leonato chastises Beatrice for being 'shrewd' of her tongue (2.1.15), he expresses the commonly held belief that women were expected to hold their tongues (keep quiet). Antonio also expresses the patriarchal assumption of male control of females when he says that he trusts Hero will be ruled by her father (2.1.38). Leonato warns Beatrice that she will not get a husband, but Beatrice defies convention by saying that she doesn't want one, and shows off her linguistic skills expressing various reasons why she won't marry. Note also the jokes about cuckoldry, through the references to horns (2.1.18; 20; 34), articulating anxieties about infidelity.

Leonato, believing that Don Pedro may woo Hero, reminds her of his counsel, demonstrating that, as Antonio suggested, daughters were generally subject to the control of their fathers, particularly in marriage matters. Hero doesn't reply and Beatrice outlines an extended analogy between relationships and dancing.

The revellers then enter and the scene comprises various vignettes: small scenes of dialogues between couples. Don Pedro woos Hero on behalf of Claudio; Hero asserts her independence and is not wholly compliant with Don Pedro's advances: 'I am yours for the walk, and especially when I walk away' (2.1.62–3). Balthasar dances with Margaret, Hero's waiting woman; and Ursula dances with Antonio, recognising him despite his mask. We then move on to the conversation between Beatrice and Benedick. Note the emphasis on negative words that start their sentences: 'No', 'Nor' and 'Not' (2.1.93–5). This conveys their antagonism in this early part of the dramatic narrative. Beatrice pretends that she does not know he is Benedick; and Benedick pretends never to have heard of himself. This provides Beatrice with the opportunity to slander him; she calls him 'the prince's jester, a very dull fool' (2.1.103).

The next pair in conversation are Don John and Claudio. Don John pretends not to recognise Claudio and asks him if he is Benedick; Claudio pretends he is Benedick. This provides Don John with the opportunity to hurt Claudio by suggesting that Don Pedro is in love with Hero, and that Hero is unworthy because she is not of equal social rank: 'she is no equal for his birth' (2.1.122–3). Once Don John and Borachio exit, Claudio's soliloquy gives the audience some insight into his feelings. When Benedick enters and tells Claudio to come with him 'for the prince hath got your Hero' (2.1.146), Claudio still reads this the wrong way. He exits, leaving Benedick to give a soliloquy, reflecting on Beatrice's comments to him.

Don Pedro enters and hears of Claudio's misunderstanding. Benedick also complains of Beatrice; the length of his speech conveys his emotions. If he had no feelings for her, he wouldn't be so hurt. The fact that he says, 'I would not marry her, though she were endowed with all that Adam had left him before he transgressed' (2.1.189–90), paradoxically suggests that he has been thinking of marriage. When Beatrice enters with the other characters, Benedick pleads with Don Pedro to send him on any minor errand, so he can escape. He uses hyperbole in suggesting various fanciful errands to the other side of the world, invoking legends about places and people beyond Europe.

Beatrice discloses that she and Benedick have had some kind of romantic relations previously, and that she feels aggrieved by it. We are not given the details; just that Beatrice feels that Benedick mistreated her.

Don Pedro tells Claudio that he has won Hero, on Claudio's behalf, and obtained Leonato's consent for the pair to be married. Claudio, however, seems tongue-tied and Beatrice, who is never short of a word, tries to encourage him to speak up. Claudio makes the wise point that if he felt less emotion then he would be able to express it (2.1.232–3). Hero is likewise unable to say anything, despite Beatrice's encouragement.

Beatrice's claim that since she is unattractive, she will 'sit in a corner' (2.1.242) and remain unwed is met by the surprising offer from Don Pedro of his hand in marriage. It is not certain how serious Don Pedro is, and directors and actors would need to decide how this episode should be played. In any event, Don Pedro takes Beatrice's refusal in a positive way, moving on from the moment by complimenting Beatrice on her merry attitude (2.1.252–3). Beatrice then exits and Don Pedro makes the observation to Leonato that Beatrice would make an excellent wife for Benedick (2.1.265). Don Pedro decides to take on the challenge of bringing Benedick and Beatrice together.

Key point

In the conversation before the masked ball begins, Beatrice claims to have 'a good eye' (2.1.59). This comment and the motif of the mask contribute to the theme of sight and the discrepancy between appearance and reality that runs throughout the play.

Q If you were a director, how would you stage 2.1 to highlight all the various conversations that take place during the dance?

Q Analyse Don Pedro's proposal to Beatrice in 2.1. How serious do you think it is, and why?

2.2 Summary: *Borachio outlines his plan to Don John to stage the appearance of a liaison between himself and Hero.*

Don John conceives of his discontent as a sickness – 'I am sick in displeasure to him' (2.2.5), suggesting that a bad deed towards Claudio will be 'medicinable' (2.2.4). Borachio outlies his plan to thwart the impending marriage by exploiting his relationship with Margaret, Hero's attendant. Note how the language carries a sense of unease: the trick will be a 'poison' (2.2.17) that will be the 'death' (2.2.16) of the marriage since Hero will seem 'contaminated' (2.2.20). This conveys the deadly potential of the plot to ruin the happiness of the lovers and irreparably damage Hero's reputation. Don John promises Borachio a considerable reward of one thousand ducats (precious coins) if he manages to pull off the trick.

2.3 Summary: *Benedick, in Leonato's orchard, overhears his companions talking of Beatrice's supposed love for Benedick. Convinced by the trick, Benedick resolves to marry Beatrice.*

Benedick's soliloquy in the orchard muses on how a man such as Claudio can scoff at others for falling in love and then fall in love himself. This is humorous as Benedick is about to experience the same thing. It is also an instance of dramatic irony as the audience knows something that the character doesn't, since we have already heard Don Pedro planning a scheme of matchmaking.

Benedick laments that Claudio used to be only interested in war, and he sets up the opposition between love and war through a series of comparisons. Firstly he uses music, comparing the 'drum and the fife' (2.3.11), the instruments of war, with the 'tabor and the pipe' (2.3.12), the courtly instruments of love; then he refers to clothes, comparing the armour of war with 'the fashion of a new doublet' (2.3.14–15); and finally he uses language, comparing the 'plain' speaking of a soldier (2.3.15) to the 'fantastical banquet' (2.3.17) of words of the lover.

Benedick then ponders on the various virtues he would expect in a wife, so his thoughts are on the topic of marriage when his companions enter to begin their trick. Although Benedick hides in the arbour, his companions are well aware he is there and they tailor their conversation to him. Don Pedro's call for music ties in with Benedick's earlier point on the shift in musical preferences with the transition from soldier to lover. Note also how the form of the speeches shifts from prose to verse from line 29 once Don Pedro, Claudio and Leonato enter. The iambic pentameter rhythm was used for sonnets which, like music, were associated with love. As Balthasar says, 'Because you talk of wooing I will sing' (2.3.41).

Don Pedro and Balthasar then have a witty conversation playing on the term 'noting', punning on the idea of noticing/seeing and musical notes. The scene is humorous on various levels since Benedick comments to himself on elements of their conversation, such as the bad singing of Balthasar, while there are also conspiratorial whispers taking place between Don Pedro, Claudio and Leonato on how the gulling is going.

Balthasar's song reflects on the inconstancy of men, which foreshadows Claudio's subsequent actions towards Hero. Note the difference between the conversation of Leonato, Claudio and Don Pedro in raised tones, intended for Benedick to hear, and the quieter tones when Claudio reflects on how the trick is progressing. Notice the various metaphors Claudio uses, from hunting ('stalk', 2.3.83), fishing ('bait the hook', 2.3.97) and disease ('th'infection', 2.3.108). The friends then list Benedick's attributes before exiting, leaving him to ponder the revelation. Now believing that she is in love with him, Benedick resolves to marry Beatrice. When Beatrice enters, Benedick now sees her through a different lens and interprets her words as if there is a hidden meaning. Beatrice is bewildered by this new attitude of Benedick's.

Key vocabulary

villainy (2.1.105): offensiveness (rather than wickedness); a villain originally meant a peasant, of the lower classes, so the derogatory nature of the term originates in class snobbery.

whither (2.1.142): where.

willow (2.1.143): tree with drooping branches; a symbol of unrequited love as the tree appears to be bowed over, weeping.

drovier (2.1.148): cattle drover or dealer.

Antipodes (2.1.200): lands in the southern hemisphere (such as Australia).

civil as an orange (2.1.223): a pun on Seville, which was renowned for its oranges.

blazon (2.1.225): description.

sunburnt (2.1.242): unattractive; pale skin was thought to be an attractive attribute for women, since being tanned was associated with labouring in the sun, and therefore with the lower classes.

temper (2.2.17): mix, concoct.

contaminated stale (2.2.20): prostitute with venereal disease.

despite (2.2.24): injure.

meet (2.2.25): suitable.

orthography (2.3.16): speaking elaborate language.

daffed (2.3.145): put aside.

if I do not love her I am a Jew (2.3.212): here the phrase 'I am a Jew' means 'I am faithless'; it is a racist slur, the basis of which is that the Jewish faith does not agree with the Christian belief that Jesus was the son of God.

Act 3

3.1 Summary: *Beatrice is now duped into believing Benedick is in love with her.*

It is now Beatrice's turn to be tricked by her companions. Hero directs Margaret to have Beatrice come to a bower in the orchard so she can overhear Hero and Ursula. The language is similar to the men's trapping of Benedick, in that they use the vocabulary of hunting and fishing: 'angling' (3.1.26), 'false sweet bait' (3.1.33) and 'limed' (3.1.104; birdlime was a sticky substance used as bait for birds). Also, as in the previous scene, there is a distinction between the conversation intended for Beatrice to hear (beginning at 3.1.36) and the private conversation between Hero and Ursula about the trick (3.1.24–36 and 3.1.104–6).

Hero's rhetorical (persuasive) strategy is to criticise Beatrice for being too proud, disdainful and self-centred, and therefore not able to love. This provides effective bait for Beatrice to want to counter it. Beatrice, like Benedick in the previous scene, quickly succumbs to the trick and, at the end of the scene, she resolves to love Benedick.

Although Hero and Ursula's deception is in a comic, playful vein, it reminds the audience that there is a more sinister plan impending. The disturbing language, such as 'greedily devour the treacherous bait' (3.1.28), resonates with what Don John and his companions will do to Claudio. Furthermore, Hero's suggestion that she will 'devise some honest slanders, / To stain my cousin with' (3.1.84–5), in order to dissuade Benedick from loving Beatrice, unwittingly foreshadows what will happen to Hero. Her language – 'stain' (3.1.85) and 'empoison' (3.1.86) – creates a sinister undertone that signals to the audience what is to come.

Key point

At the end of this scene, Beatrice's speech is not only in verse (iambic pentameter) but it also has the heroic rhyming pattern of a sonnet (*abab cdcd ee*). It is not quite a sonnet since it is ten lines, not fourteen; however, the form of the speech signals that Beatrice is also now in love.

Q How do you read Beatrice's swift shift in attitude to Benedick at the end of 3.1? Does it suggest that she already had feelings for him? Alternatively, could Shakespeare be suggesting how powerful vanity can be in creating love?

3.2 Summary: *Benedick joins his companions, now a changed man. The merry tone of the group is soured when Don John arrives with his slander of Hero.*

When Claudio offers to accompany Don Pedro to Arragon after the wedding, Don Pedro says this would 'soil' the 'new gloss' of Claudio's marriage (3.2.4); the language foreshadows the imminent stain that Don John is about to bring.

Benedick appears, announcing his new state: 'I am not as I have been' (3.2.11). He complains of toothache (holding his jaw to disguise the fact that he is newly shaven) but his friends diagnose love – his new care with his appearance a clear symptom of being in love. They note that he now brushes his hat (3.2.32) and uses perfume ('civet', 3.2.37).

The happy banter is abruptly halted by the entry of Don John, who claims that Hero has been unfaithful. By repeating Hero's name – 'Leonato's Hero, your Hero, every man's Hero' (3.2.78) – Don John suggests her promiscuity. His sly wording also subtly suggests his deception: 'think you of a worse title, and I will fit her to it' (3.2.81). That is, Don John will use Claudio's wavering trust in Hero and work to make Hero seem to fit that description. Don John is able to rely on the misogyny and general mistrust of women common in the period. He need only 'show [Claudio] enough' (3.2.89) and Claudio's fragile belief in his betrothed will do the rest.

Note in this scene the many words associated with sight: 'appear' (3.2.70), 'manifest' (3.2.71), 'see' (3.2.82; 88), 'show' (3.2.89; 96) and 'witnesses' (3.2.95). More powerful than the external, visual 'proof' of Hero's 'guilt', however, are the unspoken general assumptions about the unreliability and inconstancy of women; these attitudes and beliefs are strong enough for the men to believe Don John over Hero, despite Don John's history of antagonism towards his brother. Claudio quickly resolves not to marry Hero and to publicly 'shame her' (3.2.92) if he is convinced by Don John's evidence.

3.3 Summary: *The play switches focus to the comic characters of the Watch who, despite their general incompetence, manage to uncover the slander plot when they overhear Borachio and Conrade.*

Dogberry, a constable and employee of Leonato, tells his men how to go about the night watch. This generates humour through Dogberry's incompetence with language – his malapropisms (misused words) may sound similar to the words he intends but they often have the opposite meaning. Verges' language is also full of malapropisms. Furthermore, Dogberry's instructions seem to undermine the very purpose of the watch. If an apprehended person refuses to stop, the watch should 'let him go' (3.3.24), and sleeping on duty is fine since Dogberry 'cannot see how sleeping should offend' (3.3.35). Furthermore, if they come across a thief, they should let him go, since not having anything to do with him will reflect better on their honesty. With these nonsensical instructions, Dogberry and Verges leave Seacoal and the watchmen.

In Shakespeare's time there was no public police force as such; the upper class would employ soldiers and others to keep watch over their properties and that is the role Dogberry has. Also note how Dogberry instructs his men to arrest any vagrants. In the early modern period it was often considered a crime to be wandering homeless, and unfortunate people in this position were treated with suspicion.

Despite Dogberry's difficulties with language and poor instructions to his men, they manage to uncover the slander plot by overhearing Borachio and Conrade, and arrest them. Ironically it is by doing nothing that Seacoal and his men hear of the plot. Humour also arises when Borachio's observation that fashion is 'deformed' (3.3.102) – that is, it disguises the true nature of a person – is misunderstood by Watchman 1 as a reference to an actual person called 'Deformed' (3.3.103), a reference Dogberry continues in a later scene.

Q Analyse Dogberry's language in this scene and identify all the malapropisms. Which words does he intend to use and how do the wrong words create humour?

3.4 Summary: *In Hero's dressing room, Margaret and Ursula help dress Hero for the wedding, and the women tease Beatrice over Benedick.*

We shift to the intimate space of Hero's dressing room where the women are preparing for the wedding. The focus on clothing continues the theme of fashion from the previous scene, particularly with repetition of the word (3.4.11; 17), thus giving it an ominous undertone through its link with deception. That Hero's heart is 'heavy' (3.4.19) foreshadows the pain of the upcoming slander scene, although Margaret makes a bawdy pun on the word 'heavy', reflecting her earthier nature. Margaret's comment, 'bad thinking do not wrest true speaking' (3.4.25), also foreshadows what Hero is about to experience. Beatrice enters and the women tease her about being in love with Benedick. Beatrice is not feeling well, a state commonly associated with being in love, so Margaret prescribes 'distilled

Carduus benedictus', thus punning on Benedick's name (3.4.54). There are also jokes and puns on pregnancy: 'burden' (3.4.33); 'barns' (a homonym for 'bairns' – children, 3.4.36); and 'stuffed' (3.4.47).

3.5 Summary: *Dogberry attempts to tell Leonato about the plot but communication fails.*

In this last scene of the act, Dogberry and Verges meet Leonato to attempt to report the plot they have uncovered. However, Dogberry's longwindedness, malapropisms and misunderstandings result in the exasperated Leonato declaring, 'I would fain know what you have to say' (3.5.23). Dogberry misunderstands Leonato's description of them as 'tedious' (3.5.14), taking it as a compliment. Further humour is created when Dogberry is condescending to Verges, acting as if it is only Verges who is incompetent. Leonato, in a hurry to get to the wedding, instructs Dogberry to examine the arrested men himself. In the last line of the scene, Dogberry's mistaken use of 'excommunication' (3.5.51) instead of communication points to the missed opportunity for Leonato to be made aware of the plot prior to the wedding.

Key vocabulary

haggards (3.1.36): wild female hawks.

fight against his passion (3.1.83): what was known as 'psychomachia', a war between desire and restraint, body and mind.

requite (3.1.111): return (Benedick's) love.

vouchsafe (3.2.3): allow.

humour or a worm (3.2.21): humours (elements comprising the body) and worms were believed to reside in hollow teeth, causing toothache.

dies for him (3.2.50): a bawdy expression for an orgasm.

buried with her face upwards (3.2.51): another bawdy expression; continues the sexual innuendo of 'dies' meaning that the only 'dying' will be in bed with Benedick.

hobby-horses (3.2.54): buffoons.

holp (3.2.72): helped.

vagrom (3.3.21): vagrant; homeless.

stand close (3.3.88): be quiet.

unconfirmed (3.3.96): inexperienced.

a (3.3.104; 138): he.

troth (3.4.5): in truth.

rebato (3.4.5): wired neck ruff.

tire (3.4.10): wired headdress.

turned Turk (3.4.42): changed belief, like Turks converting from Christianity to Islam.

Act 4

4.1 Summary: *Claudio rejects Hero and publicly shames her. Hero faints and is assumed to be dead. The Friar proposes that they pretend that Hero is in fact dead, in the hope that Claudio will become remorseful. Benedick and Beatrice admit their love for each other, but Benedick's loyalty is tested when Beatrice demands that he kill Claudio as revenge.*

Everyone gathers for the wedding. However, after quibbling over language, Claudio not only rejects Hero but publicly slanders and shames her, accusing her of being unfaithful to him. He directs Leonato to 'take her back again' (4.1.26). The metaphor of the 'rotten orange' (4.1.27) has a link with prostitution since prostitutes commonly sold oranges at Shakespeare's Globe. Claudio's repetition of the word 'do' (4.1.14–15) has a bitter sexual undertone that undermines what should have been a joyful 'I do' at the wedding ceremony; the phrases also chime with the play's title.

Ironically, although Claudio believed the outward appearance of 'Hero' being unfaithful, now he does not take Hero's blushing as evidence of her innocence, instead assuming that it is only an outward show. His claim, 'Oh what authority and show of truth / Can cunning sin cover itself withal!' (4.1.30–1), reflects on the effectiveness of Don John's plot. Throughout the scene, there is an emphasis on words for seeing.

Hero questions Claudio: 'And seemed I ever otherwise to you?' (4.1.49); and Claudio paradoxically asks the rhetorical question, 'Are our eyes our own?' (4.1.65). In fact, Don John has possessed Claudio's eyes and tainted his vision.

Claudio's alliteration and playing with words – 'fare thee well, most foul, most fair, farewell' (4.1.96) – together with the chiasmus 'pure impiety, and impious purity' (4.1.97) convey the troubled state of his mind as he attempts to reconcile Hero's fair appearance with her supposed unfaithfulness. When Don John says 'these things come thus to light' (4.1.104), he is punning on 'light', which meant unchaste. His expression in 'smother her spirits up' (4.1.105) has an implication of violence; he has silenced her and killed her reputation.

Leonato, like Claudio, interprets Hero's blushing and fainting as evidence against her. Like Claudio and Don Pedro, Leonato sees Hero in the context of misogynist assumptions. His language also emphasises the idea of taint: 'smirchèd', 'mired' (4.1.126), 'pit of ink' (4.1.133) and 'foul tainted flesh' (4.1.136).

How do the other characters react? Beatrice knows Hero has been slandered as she knows Hero well. The Friar also takes a more positive attitude, correctly 'noting' (4.1.150) and reading the outward signs of Hero's reaction. These attitudes contrast with those of the three prominent males who do not react rationally. Leonato knows his daughter well yet misjudges her. Don Pedro knows the character of his brother Don John, but nevertheless believes him.

Benedick does not assume that Hero is guilty and at first suspends judgement. He then suspects Don John, assessing that if Claudio and Don Pedro are 'misled in this, / The practice of it lives in John the bastard, / Whose spirits toil in frame of villainies' (4.1.180–2). This introduces doubt to Leonato's mind. The Friar urges calm and proposes that they all pretend that Hero is dead. His idea is that this may change Claudio's attitude and cause him to value Hero once more. If that does not work, the Friar proposes the alternative course of action that Hero be sequestered in a religious institution. The implication here is that if her reputation is now ruined, she will be unable to marry and will need to live as a nun.

Benedick's loyalties are divided and they are tested once he and Beatrice are alone. Firstly, the crisis creates the opportunity for the pair to confess their love for each other. However, Beatrice immediately presents him with the brutal directive to prove his love: 'Kill Claudio' (4.1.279). The alliteration of the harsh 'k' sound emphasises the threat of violence. The scene ends with Benedick agreeing to challenge Claudio to a duel.

Key point

Note how in the ceremony Hero is treated as a piece of property owned by her father Leonato and 'given' by him to Claudio, the prospective husband. Once he thinks she has been unchaste, however, Claudio gives her 'back' to Leonato, claiming she is just a 'rotten orange' (4.1.27). In the early modern period, women were thought of as property; this is emphasised by Leonato in his repetition of 'mine' in anguish (4.1.129–31). In this scene the implicit question is what type of property Hero is – valued or worthless – but disturbingly, in either construction, she remains property, not her own person with agency.

Q Analyse Claudio's question 'Are our eyes our own?' (4.1.65). How does this resonate with the play's themes?

Q Analyse the different characters' reactions to the slander against Hero in 4.1 and what they rely on in either believing or rejecting the accusation. What do their reactions reveal about them?

4.2 Summary: *Dogberry and Verges interrogate the prisoners Conrade and Borachio; the malapropisms and problems with communication turn the examination into a comic farce.*

Dogberry begins the courtroom scene with a malapropism: 'Is our whole dissembly appeared?' (4.2.1); the use of 'dissembly' instead of 'assembly' reflects the chaos and disorder that creates the humour in this scene, while also recalling the sinister plot of Don John, since to dissemble is also to lie. As is the case throughout the play, the malapropisms link to the plot and themes.

Some of the malapropisms have the opposite meaning of what Dogberry intends. For example, he says of Borachio that he will be 'condemned into everlasting redemption' (4.2.47–8) for his actions, mistaking 'redemption' for 'damnation'. Dogberry also misunderstands the words others use. When the Sexton asks who the 'malefactors' are (4.2.3), meaning the suspects, Dogberry says that he and Verges are, which has a humorous effect. Dogberry even invents words, for example 'eftest' (4.2.30), which seems a conflation of deft, effective and fastest.

Dogberry's infirm grasp of communication and the correct procedure threatens to derail proceedings. When Seacoal reports that one of the accused called Don John a villain, Dogberry, instead of regarding it as evidence to be investigated, indignantly describes it as 'perjury' to accuse the Prince's brother (4.2.34). Dogberry also mislabels bribery as 'burglary' (4.2.42). However, even when he gets a word wrong, its meaning often resonates with what is happening. Don John's actions *are* a type of theft – of Hero's reputation and the young couple's happiness.

Ultimately the Sexton gets to the heart of the matter, particularly when he combines the evidence from the arrested pair with what he already knows: that Don John has 'secretly stolen away' (4.2.52) and that Hero was accused by Claudio and consequently 'died' (4.2.51–4). This is an example of dramatic irony, since the audience knows more than the characters in the scene, namely that Hero still lives.

Key vocabulary

catechising (4.1.72): questioning.

opinioned (4.2.56): Dogberry's malapropism for 'pinioned' (bound).

naughty (4.2.59): wicked (a stronger emphasis than is in common use now).

varlet (4.2.59): rogue, low-life.

piety (4.2.64): the quality of being religious or reverent; Dogberry's malapropism for 'impiety', sinfulness.

Act 5

5.1 Summary: *Leonato expresses his grief to his brother Antonio. Claudio seems little moved by Hero's reported death until Dogberry and Verges arrive and the slander plot is revealed. Claudio, now filled with remorse, agrees to Leonato's proposal that he marry Leonato's 'niece' (Hero in disguise).*

Leonato, in a long speech, articulates his grief, despite his brother Antonio's attempts to comfort him. Leonato's inconsolable state leads him to reflect on the inability of philosophy to ease grief. Antonio urges revenge and Leonato agrees, for his position has shifted and he now believes that Hero has been slandered.

Claudio and Don Pedro enter, and Leonato accuses Claudio of being a liar and challenges him to a duel, but Claudio refuses to fight him, since Leonato is an elderly man. Leonato tells them that Hero has died as a result of the slander and Claudio appears to be unmoved by this. There is no expression of grief from him at this point. Antonio is also angered and ready to join a fight in Hero's honour. Tensions rise in the group.

Don Pedro defends their position, stating that Hero 'was charged with nothing / But what was true' (5.1.103–4). The 'nothing' resonates with the play's title and undermines Don Pedro's point, emphasising that Hero has done nothing wrong. Benedick enters, and Claudio and Don Pedro joke that they were nearly in a fight with 'two old men' (5.1.112–13). Their joking seems callous and disrespectful of Leonato's mourning; they likely lose the audience's sympathy at this point.

Claudio and Don Pedro are expecting Benedick to be jovial and witty with them, but are surprised when Benedick is hostile, siding with Leonato's position and challenging Claudio to fight. This registers a new dimension to Benedick's character. Up until now he has been the lighthearted jester of the party, aligned with his comrades; however, now that he is in love with Beatrice, his loyalties have shifted away from the male group. Don Pedro and Claudio tease Benedick, and ask when he will marry Beatrice. 'Set the savage bull's horns on the sensible

Benedick's head' (5.1.163–4) equates marriage with being a cuckold: that is, having an unfaithful wife. The pair find it difficult to believe Benedick is serious, resorting to teasing him about marriage; at the same time, the jest ominously reinforces the slander of Hero as unfaithful. Benedick informs them that Don John has fled the court and then exits.

At this point Dogberry and Verges enter with Don John's arrested companions. Dogberry gives a muddled account, and Don Pedro parodies him by responding in a similar fashion. Since he cannot understand Dogberry – 'this learned constable is too cunning to be understood' (5.1.201–2) – Don Pedro asks Borachio and Conrade what they have done, upon which Borachio confesses to the plot, expressing remorse for his actions. This revelation moves Claudio deeply and he uses the metaphor of poison to express the effect on him.

Meanwhile Dogberry continues to miscommunicate, using the term 'plaintiffs' (5.1.222) instead of defendants, and 'reformed' (5.1.223) instead of informed. Once again, the incorrect word is relevant to the scene, in that Claudio and Don Pedro will now reform their position, and Borachio's remorse is also evidence of reform.

Leonato and Antonio re-enter with the Sexton. Although Leonato is angry with Borachio, he is more angry with Don Pedro and Claudio, emphasising their high status, using 'honourable men' (5.1.233) and 'bravely' (5.1.237) in an ironic tone to make the point that they should have known better. Claudio admits they were wrong, but claims that he sinned only 'in mistaking' (5.1.242), raising the question of his culpability. To what extent were Claudio's actions shaped by his society's attitudes towards women? To what extent is he at fault as an individual?

Leonato asks Don Pedro to rectify the wrongs by correcting public opinion in Messina; it is important to address the damage done to Hero's reputation. He also asks them to hang an epitaph on Hero's 'tomb' and sing it to her corpse. Finally, he proposes that, as compensation, Claudio agree to marry Leonato's 'niece' (in reality, Hero), to which Claudio readily agrees. Leonato also proposes to take Borachio to confess the plot to Margaret, who was an unknowing participant.

Key point

Note the shifts between verse and prose in this scene. When Claudio and Don Pedro are disrespectful of Leonato's grief, their dialogue switches from verse to prose. This shift from a higher form of language to a lower one registers the descent of Claudio and Don Pedro into responses that do not do them credit. However, after the revelation of the slander plot, Don Pedro and Claudio's speech switches back to verse; now that they realise their error, their mode of language reverts to match their high status. Dogberry and Verges' language, however, remains in the form of prose, corresponding to their lower status.

5.2 Summary: *Benedick attempts to write poetry for Beatrice but finds the rhyming difficult. Ursula announces that Hero has been proved innocent.*

Gardens are commonly associated with love in Shakespeare's work and here, in Leonato's garden, Benedick is attempting to write love poetry for Beatrice. He reads out his draft poem, which is very bad and written in iambic dimeter (a 'da DUM' rhythm with two stresses to the line). Beatrice enters and responds to his amorous moves with witty insults. At the beginning of the play, the pair showed off their wit by trading insults, yet now that they are in love they struggle to express their feelings. Ursula arrives to announce that Hero has been proved innocent and Don John revealed as the author of the plot.

5.3 Summary: *Claudio attends Hero's 'tomb', accompanied by Don Pedro, to read the epitaph he has written.*

Claudio's attendance at the (empty) tomb of Hero has a ritual effect. A lord reads the epitaph, which is in trochaic tetrameter. Tetrameter means there are four stresses to the line, while the trochaic beat (a stressed syllable followed by an unstressed syllable, e.g. '**Done** to **death** by') creates a forceful, insistent effect and emphasises the violence committed against Hero. This effect is reinforced by the alliteration. The sombre mood of Claudio's remorse is lifted when Don Pedro says it is dawn, so they should extinguish their torches (5.3.24). This shift from dark to light is symbolic of the shift in mood, in anticipation of the joyful last scene of the play. The more positive connotations are stressed by the references to the sun god 'Phoebus' (5.3.26, also known as Apollo), and to Hymen (5.3.32), the god of marriage.

5.4 Summary: *Everyone gathers at Leonato's house for the wedding; Hero and Claudio are married and reconciled. Benedick and Beatrice are proved to be in love by their sonnets written to each other and discovered by their companions. The play ends on a joyful note with Leonato proposing a dance and the news that Don John has been captured.*

Leonato instructs the women to be masked for the wedding ceremony, which returns to the motif of masking invoked at the beginning of the play with the masquerade. Benedick expresses his relief that he no longer has to fight Claudio, now that the matter has been resolved. Benedick also asks the Friar to marry him to Beatrice, although he jokes that in marrying, it will be 'to bind me, or undo me' (5.4.20). Leonato alludes to the tricking of Benedick and Beatrice when he says of Beatrice's 'eye of favour' (5.4.22) that it was Hero who 'lent her' (5.4.23) that sight. Leonato also tells Benedick that his 'eye of love' (5.4.24) towards Beatrice was a sight 'had from me' (5.4.25). These lines continue the play's theme of sight and appearances.

Claudio and Don Pedro arrive; Claudio confirms that he is prepared to marry Leonato's niece even 'were she an Ethiop' (5.4.38). This racist comment, which equates darker skin with an unattractive appearance, reflects ideas common in Shakespeare's time. When the women enter masked, Claudio asks to see the face of his bride, but Leonato refuses this until they are married. Leonato does not want to risk another failed marriage ceremony. This point is a crucial test for Claudio who is now unable to judge by appearances. He must do his duty as penance; his punishment is that he cannot choose according to his gaze. Claudio is thus put in the position of a woman, since early modern women often had little choice about who they were to marry.

The idea that women are the possessions of men remains embedded in the language. When Claudio asks, 'Which is the lady I must seize upon?' (5.4.53), although 'seize' means take as a wife, it also conveys a suggestion of physical force. Similarly, when Leonato says 'I do give you her' (5.4.54) and Claudio says 'then she's mine' (5.4.55), there is the reminder that women were property.

There is no stage direction from Shakespeare to specify the precise moment at which Hero's veil is lifted, although we can presume it would be either after Claudio states, 'I am your husband if you like of me' (5.4.59), or after Hero's statement, 'And when you loved, you were my other husband' (5.4.61), at which Claudio responds in astonishment, 'Another Hero?' (5.4.62). Note that Hero's response, 'Nothing certainer' (5.4.62), evokes the 'nothing' of the play's title, with all its connotations. Hero's description of herself in the third person – 'One Hero died defiled, but I do live' (5.4.63) – distances her new identity, with her reputation restored, from her former identity, whose reputation was tainted. Leonato emphasises this with his statement that Hero only 'died … whiles her slander lived' (5.4.66). Although the scene is now joyful, these lines remind us of the dark undercurrent of thought that considers a 'fallen' woman as one whose life has effectively ended.

The scene's attention then turns to Benedick and Beatrice, and the revelation of the plot to set them up threatens to derail their courtship. However, their companions step in to assert that the couple really do love each other. Claudio points to the evidence of Benedick's 'halting sonnet' to Beatrice (5.4.87); although it is poor poetry, it reveals his true feelings. Hero produces similar evidence from Beatrice's pocket. To this Benedick responds, 'here's our own hands against our hearts' (5.4.91); their writing from the heart argues against their tendency to argue in their speech.

Leonato proposes a dance to celebrate, and the play in Shakespeare's time would most likely have ended in a dance, as was common theatrical practice. The play concludes with the joyful news that Don John has been captured and brought back to Messina to face punishment.

Key vocabulary

candle-wasters (5.1.18): people who study late into the night (using a lot of candles).

dissembler (5.1.53): liar.

trial of a man (5.1.66): trial by combat; duel.

scambling (5.1.93): unruly, arguing.

out-facing (5.1.93): vain, swaggering.

fashion-monging (5.1.93): fashion-conscious, vain.

go anticly (5.1.95): dress grotesquely.

care killed a cat (5.1.127): a proverb warning against worrying too much.

give him another staff, this last was broke cross (5.1.131): a sign of cowardice in jousting; Claudio admonishes Benedick for not making them laugh.

epitaph (5.1.251): funeral poem/writing.

Leander (5.2.23): a figure from Greek mythology who had to swim the Hellespont (the Dardanelles, a strait in Turkey) to meet up with his beloved, also named Hero.

Troilus (5.2.24): a legendary figure from the Trojan War; a main character in Shakespeare's *Troilus and Cressida* (1602).

carpet-mongers (5.2.25): men who are frequently in women's bedrooms; ladies' men.

in festival terms (5.2.31): for public display (publicly reading poetry).

die in thy lap (5.2.78): sexual connotation – to 'die' meant to orgasm.

guerdon of (5.3.5): recompense for.

Q Why does Claudio initially fail to express any sorrow over Hero's death? What are the implications of this?

Q How culpable is Claudio? See if you can argue both for and against his actions.

CHARACTERS & RELATIONSHIPS

Beatrice

Key quotes

'… to be merry, best becomes you, for out a question, you were born in a merry hour.' (Don Pedro, 2.1.252–3)

'Thou and I are too wise to woo peaceably.' (Benedick, 5.2.54)

Beatrice is a lively and engaging character. She is feisty and outspoken in an era when women were supposed to be quiet, letting men dominate the conversation. Beatrice's speech is striking; she commands the first scene, demonstrating her wit and making enquiries of the messenger as if she, not Leonato, was in charge. Beatrice is sometimes described as having masculine traits, or characteristics that were more often associated with men. For example, when Benedick complains that Beatrice 'speaks poniards' (2.1.187) to him, this suggests that Beatrice is like a soldier, and her verbal barbs are like a military attack.

Her key relationship is with Benedick. Even in the first scene there are clues about her feelings. The first person she asks after is Benedick; given that there has just been military action, in asking whether he is there she can find out whether he has survived. When she states that she knows Benedick of old, we find out that they have had some form of relationship previously. Beatrice confesses that Benedick 'lent it [his heart] me a while, and I gave him use for it, a double heart for his single one: marry once before he won it of me, with false dice, therefore your grace may well say I have lost it' (2.1.211–13). This hurt accounts for the insults she constantly trades with Benedick. Her true feelings for Benedick become apparent when she is tricked by her companions in 3.1 and, despite her earlier protestations, quickly changes her stance: 'And Benedick, love on, I will requite thee' (3.1.111).

Although we associate Beatrice with a merry, high-spirited nature, a darker, steely side emerges after Hero's slander when she demands of

Benedick that he kill Claudio. She also wishes that she were a man, since then she could take revenge into her own hands (4.1.292). The different facets of Beatrice, such as her merry wit, nonconformity and fierce loyalty to Hero, all contribute to her strength and appeal as a character.

Key point

The characters of Beatrice and Benedick are often considered to have been an inspiration for Jane Austen in creating her characters of Elizabeth and Darcy in *Pride and Prejudice*. Paradoxically, it is the verbal sparring that conveys the interest they have in each other, and demonstrates their suitability in that they are equally matched in intelligence and wit. Their focus on the other person betrays their interest.

Benedick

Key quotes

'Will your grace command me any service to the world's end? I will go on the slightest errand now to the Antipodes ... rather than hold three words conference with this Harpy ...' (2.1.199–204)

'No, the world must be peopled. When I said I would die a bachelor, I did not think I should live till I were married ...' (2.3.197–8)

Benedick, like Beatrice, is clever and witty in his conversation – essential skills for a courtier. He is adept at giving insults, although perhaps Beatrice gains the upper hand in most of their verbal battles. In the first scene, Benedick, in responding to Claudio's question of whether Hero is the fairest, seems to suggest that, if Beatrice wasn't possessed by a fury, she would in fact be more beautiful than Hero (1.1.141–2). Here is the first clue about what Benedick really feels. Later, smarting from Beatrice's insults, he claims he 'would not marry her, though she were endowed with all that Adam had left him before he transgressed' (2.1.189–90). Given that he claims he dislikes her, why does he bring up the issue of marriage? Such references set up the audience's expectation that there is more to this denial. Indeed, when Benedick is tricked by his companions at the end of 2.3, once he is convinced that 'this can be no trick' (2.3.181) and that Beatrice loves him, he quickly decides he will reciprocate: 'Why, it must be requited' (2.3.183–4).

Benedick is a soldier who, like his companions Don Pedro and Claudio, has been involved in the recent conflict. His loyalty to his companions is tested when Claudio slanders Hero, and Don Pedro supports Claudio. Benedick must then choose between his new attachment to Beatrice and his loyalty to Claudio and Don Pedro. To his credit, he does not assume that Hero is guilty and, although reluctant, agrees to Beatrice's demand to challenge Claudio. Shakespeare shows how love creates change in various social relations; new relationships inevitably change pre-existing loyalties.

As an audience, we often feel close to Benedick's character because he frequently reflects on his experiences, and we often feel that we are sharing his thoughts. We see his vulnerable side, such as his hurt at Beatrice's insults, or his difficulty in writing sonnets, and this quality, together with his intelligence, makes him the perfect companion for Beatrice.

Claudio

Key quotes

'Silence is the perfectest herald of joy, I were but little happy if I could say, how much!' (2.1.232–3)

'Yet I must speak, choose your revenge yourself,
Impose me to what penance your invention
Can lay upon my sin, yet sinned I not,
But in mistaking.' (5.1.239–42)

Claudio seems at first to be a likeable character but many of his beliefs and decisions seem misguided, and by the end of the play the audience may well have a negative view of him. The first characteristic we associate with Claudio is a certain shallowness. He doesn't know Hero well when he decides he wants to marry her, and although he had seen Hero previously, before the military campaign, it is only now, with the changed circumstances of peacetime, that his thoughts turn to amorous pursuits. His feelings seem to be a product, at least in part, of the circumstances, rather than of a genuine love for Hero. His attraction appears to be superficial as he seems to fall in love with her from a distance, and with her appearance rather than her personality.

Claudio is also hampered in the wooing process because Don Pedro proposes to woo in Claudio's place. Claudio's lack of self-confidence, and the difficult situation of Don Pedro wooing on his behalf, gives rise to the first misunderstanding. Claudio becomes jealous and thinks that Don Pedro in fact has wooed Hero for himself. This foreshadows Claudio's subsequent jealousy, misunderstanding and tendency to jump to conclusions, rather than weighing up the evidence carefully.

When Claudio believes Hero to have been unfaithful, he insists that Leonato 'take her back again' (4.1.26), humiliating and slandering her at the wedding. His actions are particularly vindictive because he waits until the actual ceremony to call off the wedding. If the slander plot had not been discovered, Claudio's actions would have ruined Hero's reputation and her chances of marrying. Claudio also seems to be little affected when told of her death. Once he believes her to be tainted, whether she lives or dies seems to be of little consequence to him.

Claudio relies on surface appearances. His love seems to depend on his perception of Hero's purity. Only once Hero's innocence is revealed does his love for her return. He claims, 'Sweet Hero, now thy image doth appear / In the rare semblance that I loved it first (5.1.220–1). Ironically, as part of his repentance, Claudio has to marry without any appearance on which to form a judgement. In the end, he is rewarded by receiving the bride he wanted in the first place. Claudio expresses his remorse to Leonato, saying his fault was in mistaking an appearance for a reality; however, the audience can see that certain character flaws, as well as societal pressures, contributed to that mistake.

Key point

The relationship between Claudio and Hero has much less depth than Beatrice and Benedick's. They do not communicate well, and we learn little of their true feelings, although Claudio makes the point that his overwhelming emotion, at his engagement, is the reason he is tongue-tied. Claudio also lacks perception in reading the world around him. When at the masked ball Don John tells him that Don Pedro is in love with Hero, Claudio immediately believes this (2.1.130), in contrast to Leonato who, when he is told this in Act 1, doesn't leap to conclusions but waits for evidence.

Don Pedro

Key quotes

'Will you have me, lady?' (2.1.248)

'And as I wooed for thee to obtain her, I will join with thee, to disgrace her.' (3.2.93–4)

The relationship between Don Pedro and Leonato shifts throughout the play. At first, it is based on duty. Don Pedro, a Spanish prince and military leader, is entitled to hospitality from Leonato, since Spain ruled Sicily at the time (Italy would not become an independent and unified country until 1860). Leonato provides food, lodging and entertainment for his 'guests'. Leonato and Don Pedro are affable, courteous characters and initially they converse in a polite and friendly way. Relations sour after Claudio's false accusations against Hero. Don Pedro aligns his position with Claudio since he also witnesses the staged scene of 'infidelity'. However, Don Pedro, as a more mature person who has knowledge of his brother's nature, has more responsibility to weigh up the evidence, since it originates with Don John.

The play suggests that Don Pedro may be secretly in love with Beatrice. When Don Pedro and his companions are baiting Benedick, claiming that Beatrice has feelings for Benedick, Don Pedro says 'I would she had bestowed this dotage on me, I would have daffed all other respects, and made her half myself' (2.3.144–5). Although this is in the context of the gulling scene, there may be real feeling underneath.

Leonato

Key quote

'For there was never yet philosopher,
That could endure the tooth-ache patiently …' (5.1.35–6)

When Leonato in the first act believes that Don Pedro may be interested in marrying his daughter Hero, he counsels Hero on what to say. Don Pedro has significant social standing as a prince and a military leader, and it would be a good match for his daughter. Once Claudio and Hero are engaged, relations are cordial between Don Pedro and Leonato; however, that changes once Claudio has shamed Hero. Leonato is embarrassed and reverts to the common hostility towards 'fallen' women. He expresses the idea that his daughter's death would be preferable to the dishonour of her shame (4.1.109). This distorted logic is based on the flawed construction of women as property.

That the ruined reputation of women is a type of social death is evident in Leonato's protracted mourning speech at the beginning of Act 5, in which he reflects on his grief and how philosophy does not help. In the early modern period there were many popular works that sought to provide philosophical comfort. *The Consolation of Philosophy* by the classical writer Boethius was one such work; religious writings and collections of popular proverbs and homilies provided other sources. Leonato says that it is useless to try to 'patch grief with proverbs' (5.1.17); that is, rational thought is no help for powerful emotions. However, ironically, Leonato's speech is full of literary devices and is expressed in the style of many of the proverbs he rejects, rendering his expression of grief contrived, rather than authentic and raw. For example, he uses a simile when he says that Antonio's counsel is as useless 'as water in a sieve' (5.1.5), and personification when he says 'make misfortune drunk / With candle-wasters' (5.1.17–18).

Leonato is also wise and, at the second wedding ceremony, insists that Claudio marry the veiled bride before he sees her. This shows an awareness of Claudio's character as well as an understanding that, because Hero has been publicly slandered, this will be her only chance to marry and recover her honour.

Don John

Key quotes

'I had rather be a canker in a hedge, than a rose in his grace, and it better fits my blood to be disdained of all, than to fashion a carriage to rob love from any.' (1.3.20–2)

'He is of a very melancholy disposition.' (Hero, 2.1.5)

Don John has parallels with characters from other Shakespeare plays, such as Iago in *Othello* and Edmund in *King Lear*. Don John is antisocial and makes no attempt to be in anyone's good graces. He is clearly an outsider, which stems primarily from his status as illegitimate. In a society that was obsessive about legitimate bloodlines, so that property could pass to the rightful heirs, a 'bastard' (a child whose parents are unmarried) was ostracised and suffered prejudice. Particularly at the upper levels of society, illegitimacy meant exclusion from inheritance and recognition. In Shakespeare's plays, and others from the early modern period, characters who are illegitimate are often associated with negative characteristics, reflecting this aspect of society. Don John's resentment at his exclusion fuels his desire to ruin the happiness of Claudio, of whom he is jealous, and in doing so to act against Don Pedro, who has all the entitlement of legitimacy.

Don John claims that he is 'not of many words' (1.1.116); this renders him difficult for other characters to read. Since he says little, they cannot know what he is thinking. Yet, he also claims: 'I cannot hide what I am' (1.3.10), which is intriguing in a play about deceptive appearances.

Hero

Hero has the name of a figure from Greek mythology: a priestess of Aphrodite/Venus, the goddess of love, and the beloved of Leander. At first glance, Shakespeare's Hero seems a fairly shallow character. She does not seem to be assertive; and is not outspoken like her cousin Beatrice, particularly in mixed company. Yet, there is strength in Hero. When Don Pedro converses with her in order to woo her for Claudio, Hero does not agree straight away. She is witty and asserts her right to reject him, although this is a limited right, given Don Pedro's status and Leonato's obligations. When she is only with her female companions, she speaks more freely, and she takes an active role in the gulling of Beatrice, and in producing the secret sonnet that proves Beatrice's love for Benedick.

In one sense Hero functions as an abstract idea in the play: that of reputation ruined and then restored. She undergoes a symbolic death and resurrection yet, as well as having this traumatic narrative arc, Hero is instrumental in bringing Beatrice and Benedick together.

Dogberry

Dogberry is one of Leonato's constables, responsible for keeping the peace. His lack of education results in him constantly using malapropisms – incorrect words that sound similar to the words he intends. Dogberry is a source of much humour in the play. When he is slandered by Conrade, Dogberry, in expressing his outrage at the insult, inadvertently emphasises its validity, and appears to be endorsing it, claiming 'But masters, remember that I am an ass' (4.2.62–3). Although he is incompetent, Dogberry is ironically successful at uncovering the slander plot.

THEMES, IDEAS & VALUES

Appearances versus truth

Key quotes

'... I will so fashion the matter, that Hero shall be absent, and there shall appear such seeming truth of Hero's disloyalty, that jealousy shall be called assurance, and all the preparation overthrown.' (Borachio, 2.2.34–37)

'Are our eyes our own?' (Claudio, 4.1.65)

The gap between surface appearances and truth, between what things seem to be and what they are, is a central theme of the play, in both positive and negative aspects. Claudio truly believes he sees Hero in the embrace of another. The illusion is effective firstly because he is being manipulated by Don John, and so already suspects Hero is unfaithful before he sees the visual 'evidence'. However, the illusion is also effective because of the prevalent misogynistic views of the time, which regarded women as by nature unreliable and susceptible to seduction.

The masked ball in the first act draws attention to the theme of disguise. The masks enable characters to talk and interact more freely, and the unknown identities create mystery and intrigue. Disguise also enables Beatrice to insult Benedick, while pretending that she doesn't know it is him. The theme of the mask returns at the end of the play when Claudio must accept a masked bride, agreeing to marry her even though he knows nothing about her. This is a reminder that Claudio at the beginning of the play wanted to marry Hero without really knowing anything about her.

The manipulation of appearances is double-edged. It is for a positive outcome in the case of Benedick and Beatrice. The deception that the other has declared their love (which is arguably true, albeit unknown to the pair) pleases their ego, so the tricks facilitate them coming together. On the other hand, illusion is used for a negative purpose by Don John against Claudio and Hero. Ultimately, their relationship needs to be fixed by a further trick whereby Claudio believes he is marrying an unknown bride, and is married to Hero in disguise. Claudio, believing Hero to be dead, must agree to marry someone he hasn't seen. Thus he must be paradoxically tricked into marrying someone he actually wants to marry.

In exploring the discrepancy between appearance and truth, Shakespeare also makes the important point that we see what we want or expect to see; the mind shapes and influences what we see. When Benedick in the orchard is wondering at the transformation of Claudio from soldier to lover, he also ponders whether he himself would be capable of such a transformation: 'may I be so converted and see with these eyes?' (2.3.18). He is alluding to the fact that a lover sees the world, and his beloved, through a particular set of eyes, and of course by the end of the scene Benedick's vision has been likewise converted. Once he believes Beatrice to be in love with him at the end of 2.3, when she enters, Benedick claims 'I do spy some marks of love in her' (2.3.199–200).

Key point

Shakespeare is making the point that our thoughts frame what we see; we see what our mind is already looking for or expecting.

The discussion about fashion between Borachio and Conrade in 3.3 also explores the gap between appearance and truth. As Borachio points out, what a person wears is not the person themselves: 'the fashion of a doublet, or a hat, or a cloak, is nothing to a man' (3.3.96–7). The deceptive nature of outer garments, which can mistakenly be read as a reflection of a person's character, makes fashion, in Borachio's view, a 'deformed thief' (3.3.102). This is, in fact, an apt description of Don John who, although dressed 'like a gentleman' (3.3.104), is a 'vile thief' (3.3.103) who deceives Claudio and steals Hero's reputation. Although Conrade chides Borachio for getting off topic by talking about fashion, Borachio points to its relevance, since Margaret was manipulated to be mistaken for Hero, the outer appearance disguising the truth.

The ideas of 'noting', of observing, of drawing information from the eyes and of the fallibility of appearances, are central to the play. All are invoked in the concept of surveillance. Dogberry, head of the night watch, is hired to guard the town of Messina. The early modern period was a time of much violence, and there was no effective system of policing, as there is in modern times. We know that Don Pedro and his company have recently been involved in military action, so there is a real threat of conflict within the vicinity. Although Dogberry is on the lookout for external threats, what the play reveals is that threats are often internal. It is not a military army that threatens Leonato but the poisonous slander initiated by Don John.

We do not see the scene in which Claudio and Don Pedro are deceived. Instead we hear about it from Borachio's account in 3.3. He describes how Claudio and Don Pedro were 'planted, and placed, and possessed' (3.3.122) in a particular location in the orchard so that the deceptive appearance of Borachio wooing 'Hero' would be convincing. What they saw, as Borachio recognises, was a combination of three elements: Don John's slander 'which first possessed them' (3.3.127–8), the dark night, and Borachio's deceptive performance. Thus their sight was framed so their 'noting' made something of 'nothing'. There is thus much ado over an illusion, a nothing.

Language

Key quotes

'I would fain know what you have to say.' (Leonato, 3.5.23)

'One word, sir, our watch, sir, have indeed comprehended two aspitious persons, and we would have them this morning examined before your worship.' (Dogberry, 3.5.35–7)

'... marry, I cannot show it in rhyme, I have tried ... No, I was not born under a rhyming planet, nor I cannot woo in festival terms.' (Benedick, 5.2.27–31)

The use of language is a key theme of the play. For the courtiers, language is necessary to display wit, intelligence and linguistic abilities. Skilful use of language was considered to be an essential attribute of the courtier and for every use of language for which the purpose is to communicate, there is an additional motive of impressing superiors and companions. This doesn't apply to everyone, however. Don John claims that he is a man of few words and he does not seek to be in good favour with Don Pedro.

Throughout the play, words are shown to be particularly powerful. Language can communicate or miscommunicate. Words may be violent; insults traded by Beatrice and Benedick are weapons that wound, even as they are funny for the audience. Rhetoric (persuasive language) can manipulate a person's views or even ways of seeing, as Don John's powerful slander is shown to do. This leads to Claudio's slander of Hero, which is such a powerful weapon that Hero appears to 'die' from the wound to her reputation. Among the lower-class characters, the slander of Dogberry, when Conrade calls him an ass, echoes that of Hero, creating a comic parallel to the main plot. The wound that this insult inflicts on Dogberry is evident in his insistence on recording it in the court leger, and in returning to the issue in a later scene.

In contrast to the skilful use of language by most of the characters, we have the comic figure of Dogberry who uses words incorrectly. Not only are his words often incorrect but they commonly have the opposite meaning to what he intends. For example, in 3.3, Dogberry instructs his men to 'comprehend all vagrom men' (3.3.21), meaning he wants them to apprehend all vagrant men. The incorrect word 'comprehend' is particularly humorous as it reflects ironically on the difficulty of comprehending what Dogberry means. Leonato becomes particularly frustrated in 3.5 when trying to ascertain what Dogberry is trying to tell him. In Shakespeare's period, many people did not receive an education, although Shakespeare himself was fortunate to have gone to the local grammar school in Stratford. Dogberry has clearly not received a thorough education. Yet we generally understand what he is trying to say from the context of the sentence and other dialogue that surrounds the incorrect word.

In the first scene in which we meet Dogberry and his men, they discuss reading and writing. Dogberry appoints George Seacoal as constable on the basis of his education, even though Dogberry mistakenly refers to this as 'nature' (3.3.14) when he means nurture. Dogberry actually cuts off Seacoal before he can confirm whether he can read and write, thus Dogberry's labelling of him as 'senseless' (when he means sensible, 3.3.19) may in fact be accurate.

Another aspect of language in the play is the association between love and poetry, which reflects the practice at the time of channelling the strong emotions of love, particularly unrequited love, into poetry. Benedick, once he accepts that he is in love with Beatrice, attempts to write a sonnet for her, but finds it difficult to think of rhymes that go beyond cliché. Shakespeare was a gifted poet, so Benedick's struggle with the formal requirements of a sonnet offers a window onto the challenges that Shakespeare regularly engaged with (although with considerably more skill than Benedick!).

Key point

As you read the play, keep an eye out for 'soundbites', short statements with advice on how to live. One such example is: 'happy are they that hear their detractions, and can put them to mending' (2.3.187–8). Another example occurs when the Friar reflects on the human tendency to not appreciate what we have: 'That what we have, we prize not to the worth, / Whiles we enjoy it; but being lacked and lost, / Why then we rack the value, then we find / The virtue that possession would not show us / Whiles it was ours' (4.1.211–15). Audiences of the time may have written these sorts of statements in their commonplace books, which held collections of notable quotations and epigrams.

Love and conflict

Key quote

'... there is a kind of merry war betwixt Signor Benedick and her: they never meet but there's a skirmish of wit between them.' (Leonato, 1.1.45–7)

In *Much Ado*, the themes of love and war are tied together. Don Pedro and his soldiers have been involved in a military campaign when they arrive at Messina, and at the end of the first scene, Claudio talks of how his thoughts have turned from war to love. Yet something of the nature of war appears to cross over and affect how the characters negotiate love. Disturbingly, Don Pedro's language at the end of 1.1, when he proposes to woo Hero on Claudio's behalf, is full of the imagery of war. He will 'take her hearing prisoner with the force / And strong encounter of [his] amorous tale' (1.1.250–1). These violent undertones do not suggest a good start to his wooing.

Then there is the tempestuous journey of Beatrice and Benedick from animosity to love; their relationship is described in the first scene as a 'merry war' (1.1.45–6). Their seemingly good-natured antagonism masks the hurt they feel from previous encounters with each other, and the play suggests that in the past there was some potential of attachment that went astray.

Another type of conflict suggested is an internal war. Leonato, during the tricking of Benedick, refers to a war within Beatrice where there is 'wisdom and blood combating' (2.3.140). This was known as psychomachia, a war of the mind, usually between desire and chastity. The union of Benedick and Beatrice at the end of the play has to be brought about by a trick orchestrated by their friends, forcing each of them to reveal their true feelings, which were perhaps hidden even from themselves.

Also note how, in the aftermath of Hero's slander, Beatrice asks Benedick to kill Claudio. Benedick, although torn by conflicting loyalties to his new love and to his fellow soldiers, challenges Claudio to a duel (which never occurs, since the conflict is resolved). A duel was often fought to defend a point of honour or as the result of a perceived insult. In this case, Benedick is challenging Claudio to defend Hero's honour.

Key point

Shakespeare conveys the way in which interactions between people are often full of tension and conflict that must be negotiated and resolved. He also explores the link between love and war in other plays, especially those in the tragic genre, such as *Romeo and Juliet*, *Othello* and *Antony and Cleopatra*.

Marriage

Key quotes

'I had rather hear my dog bark at a crow than a man swear he loves me.' (Beatrice, 1.1.97–8)

'I will live a bachelor.' (Benedick, 1.1.182)

'Sigh no more, ladies, sigh no more,
Men were deceivers ever,
One foot in sea, and one on shore,
To one thing constant never.' (Balthasar, 2.3.53–6)

Paradoxically, *Much Ado* presents marriage as something to be both desired and avoided. In fact, the play seems to stage a kind of debate on the merits of marriage. Shakespeare's education included having to debate a topic from multiple perspectives, and this trait is often reflected in his work.

At the beginning of the play, both Beatrice and Benedick claim they will never marry. Beatrice claims that, after she dies and goes to heaven, St Peter will show her 'where the bachelors sit, and there live we, as merry as the day is long' (2.1.36–7). At the masked ball, she uses an extended simile likening the different stages of 'wooing, wedding, and repenting' (2.1.52–3) to various kinds of dancing. Similarly, in 2.3, Benedick believes he is safe from matrimony unless a woman combines all virtues in one person. He then lists all the attributes he requires. Thus, he engages in a hypothetical exercise in what he would be seeking in a wife, which hints to the audience that underneath his denials he is in fact thinking about matrimony. At the end, once happily engaged to Beatrice, Benedick advises Don Pedro to 'get thee a wife' (5.4.115).

When Claudio seems to fall in love with Hero at first sight, marriage is what he strongly desires. Yet, once he believes Hero to be 'tainted', he wants to avoid marriage. Fear of female infidelity and a deep insecurity about being able to possess women lie at the heart of the cuckoldry jokes throughout the play. The male characters constantly link marriage with infidelity. While Antonio exits to bring in Hero at the second wedding ceremony, Claudio teases Benedick about getting married and becoming a cuckold (5.4.43–7), invoking the myth of Jove and Europa, in which the god disguised himself as a bull in order to abduct the nymph Europa. Benedick retorts with a similar horn-themed jibe (5.4.48–51), suggesting that Claudio's mother was unfaithful and Claudio is therefore illegitimate. The joking is a strange theme to enter into just prior to the wedding ceremony, touching as it does on the painful recent events of the slander of Hero. However, in Shakespeare's time, the notion of the cuckold was one of the common jokes surrounding the idea of marriage, and is commonly found in the banter between men across Shakespeare's plays. Even in the joyful final moments of the play, after Claudio and Hero are reunited, and Benedick is engaged to Beatrice, Claudio returns to the theme of infidelity, claiming that Benedick will likely prove a 'double dealer' (5.4.109) – unfaithful.

On the subject of infidelity, it is interesting to consider the song of Balthasar in 2.3. His song suggests that, contrary to the assertions of the men throughout the play and the common early modern assumptions of female infidelity, it is men who are inconstant and deceptive. The song, in fact, advises women not to tie themselves to men if they want to be free and happy. Of course, none of the characters take any notice of this, and the play ends with a wedding and an engagement. Yet the audience cannot be certain that these marriages will be strong, since that of Claudio and Hero begins with a traumatic event; and Benedick and Beatrice had to be tricked into believing the other loved them.

Key point

Benedick's first requirement in a wife (expressed in 2.3), that she be rich, seems a shallow basis on which to choose a partner. However, it reflects the realities of the early modern marriage market for the upper classes, with marriage often treated in the manner of a commercial transaction: parents chose partners for their offspring on the basis of wealth and social standing.

Gender

Key quotes

'... why she, oh she is fallen
Into a pit of ink, that the wide sea
Hath drops too few to wash her clean again,
And salt too little, which may season give
To her foul tainted flesh.' (Leonato, 4.1.132–6)

'Oh that I were a man!' (Beatrice, 4.1.292)

In Shakespeare's time, both women and men were constricted by gender roles and expectations, and this is reflected in the play. Women were expected to be chaste, silent and obedient. Verbal wit was supposed to be the province of men, yet Beatrice is commonly the centre of any conversation when she is on stage. Leonato chastises Beatrice for being too outspoken: 'By my troth, niece, thou wilt never get thee a husband, if thou be so shrewd of thy tongue' (2.1.14–15). The assumption is that a man will only want a wife who is submissive and doesn't speak her mind, so that he can retain power over her. Women were also expected to obey men. Antonio says to Beatrice: 'I trust you will be ruled by your father' (2.1.38), but Beatrice shows little inclination for this. She claims she will not marry, which again resists societal pressures for women.

Men assumed their dominance over women in the period because women had few legal rights and were considered the property of their fathers and then their husbands. The slander of Hero demonstrates the ways in which women were thought of as property and their reputations were vulnerable. There was a double standard in place because there were no such restrictions on men's sexuality.

According to the biblical story of the Fall, it was Eve who fell first, tempting Adam just as the serpent had tempted her. There is also a long history of biblical exegesis (critical interpretation) and of writings by the Church fathers that viewed women as linked with sin and temptation. In the early modern period these ideas retained power; men were assumed to be more rational while women were associated with the body and assumed to be more likely to be unfaithful. Women's sexuality had, in this view of gender roles and identity, to be controlled and contained through marriage.

Leonato's misguided view in 4.1 that Hero is better dead than 'shamed' creates the dark vein of the play and arises from the distorted thinking of women as property. The idea that death is preferable to dishonour can be seen throughout Shakespeare's Roman plays and his poem 'The Rape of Lucrece'. Tragically, this thinking still exists in some societal contexts today, giving rise to so-called 'honour killings', resulting in the deaths of many young women.

DIFFERENT INTERPRETATIONS

Different interpretations arise from different responses to a text. Over time, a text will evoke a wide range of responses from its readers, who may come from various social or cultural groups and live in very different places and historical periods. Responses by critics and reviewers can be published in newspapers, journals and books, both online and in print. They can also be expressed in discussions among readers in the media, classrooms, book groups and so on.

While there is no single correct reading or interpretation of a text, it is important to understand that an interpretation is more than a personal opinion – it is the justification of a point of view on the text. To present an interpretation of a text based on your point of view, you must use a logical argument and support it with relevant evidence from the text.

The critics' viewpoints

Literary criticism, often referred to as 'secondary sources', is a form of writing about a text, the 'primary source'. Literary critics, in writing about a text, are entering into a dialogue with other critics and so try to take into account differing opinions. Since Shakespeare's work has been around for a long time, there is a substantial amount of critical material about his plays and poetry. This can be daunting for students and critics alike. Whether you are expected to research some literary criticism as part of your study of the play will depend on your level of study and the expectations of your teacher. If you do need to consider this, keep in mind that it is not possible for anyone to read and understand everything that is relevant to the play. Try to select a few articles or book sections that discuss an area of interest to you. Reading literary criticism should be enjoyable and is intended to help you order your thoughts and shape your own ideas about the play. It can also open your eyes to aspects of the play that you hadn't noticed.

Different interpretations of the play are also made every time it is produced on stage or as a film. A particular production constitutes an interpretation because directors, script editors, cinematographers and others make choices, such as to cut, add or rearrange lines and scenes. Choices are also made regarding costumes, sets, casting, props, music, sound and visual effects, all of which create varying interpretations of the play. Actors bring interpretive decisions to their performances, and audiences will bring their own experiences to the play and respond to it in subjective ways.

In terms of approaching *Much Ado* from the perspective of genre, some valuable insights can be found in *The Cambridge Introduction to Shakespeare's Comedies* (Gay 2008). This will assist you to think about aspects relevant to *Much Ado* as well as issues common to all of Shakespeare's comedies.

Many scholarly editions of the play provide a helpful introduction and overview, considering themes, historical contexts and aspects of characterisation; they provide summaries of the different approaches taken by critics and examine stage and film histories. These can provide a useful starting point for determining which aspects of the play you wish to research. *The Norton Shakespeare* has a comprehensive introduction to *Much Ado* by Stephen Greenblatt that covers all of the key aspects of the play and a relevant list of recommended readings. Also look at the excellent materials in the Oxford School Shakespeare edition (2014), aimed at secondary school students, and the Arden performance edition edited by Anna Kamaralli (2018). It is also worth looking at edited collections of essays, which provide a range of different perspectives, rather than just one critic's viewpoint. An excellent example is *Much Ado About Nothing: A Critical Reader* (Cartmell & Smith 2018).

Much Ado raises various issues that have been explored throughout its critical history. In seeking an overview of these diverse issues, an excellent starting place is Marjorie Garber's chapter on the play in her *Shakespeare After All* (2004). Garber describes it as 'Shakespeare's great play about gossip. Everything is overheard, misheard, or constructed on purpose for eavesdropping' and she makes valuable observations on the theme of 'noting' in the play (p.375, pp.379–80). Nova Myhill (1999) also explores the theme of unreliable 'noting' in the play, and Benjamin C Lockerd (2011) provides valuable historical contexts in examining how sight is presented in *Much Ado*, compared with *King Lear*.

Steve Cassal draws attention to the fact that there are two slanders in the play and points out that Dogberry's defamation resembles Hero's, and that both are vulnerable figures in Messina (Cassal 2006, p.139). Joost Daalder (2004) examines the play's hints at the 'pre-history' of Benedick and Beatrice's relationship, and compares the characters of Benedick and Claudio as young men in love.

When using the internet for research, aim to use peer-reviewed sites. An excellent place to start for *Much Ado* is the Internet Shakespeare Editions series site on the play (Minton & Werier 2019). This has a wealth of information including introductory essays, with an in-depth outline of the play's critical reception, historical information and images, discussion of questions raised by the play and information on stage productions. If you are researching a particular issue and your library has access to databases, use the *MLA International Bibliography* and the *Literature Online* databases. These will allow you to enter search terms and find scholarly articles on your topic.

Two interpretations

Any text is open to contrasting, yet equally valid, interpretations. Here are two different perspectives on whether in *Much Ado About Nothing* Shakespeare challenges or affirms early modern assumptions about women.

Interpretation 1: *Much Ado About Nothing* challenges assumptions about women.

In the early modern period, women were expected to be chaste, silent and obedient. In *Much Ado About Nothing*, Shakespeare challenges these various constructions and expectations. In relation to speech, the public sphere was thought to belong to men. Women were not expected to voice their opinion. Beatrice, however, is outspoken and independent. She engages in a 'merry war' (1.1.45–6) with Benedick, and her insults, as he admits, can wound: 'she speaks poniards, and every word stabs' (2.1.187). Even once she is united with Benedick, there is no suggestion that Beatrice will become less feisty and outspoken. She and Benedick will likely have lively conversations and a marriage of educated minds.

Beatrice, as an orphan who relies on her uncle for support, is socially and economically vulnerable. She will not inherit money, as Hero will. This makes her initial stance against marriage brave and a sign of her independence. Her uncle Leonato wishes her to marry, and if Beatrice were obedient then she would not so readily reject Don Pedro when he asks, 'Will you have me, lady?' (2.1.248). Given Don Pedro's high status and Beatrice's economic vulnerability, this shows her refusal to meekly conform. Other behaviours more commonly associated with masculinity that Beatrice demonstrates include her direction to Benedick to 'Kill Claudio' (4.1.279); women were expected to be passive and nurturing, not violent. Nor were they expected to direct men. In Beatrice's actions, Shakespeare is presenting an unconventional female character.

Not only does Shakespeare reward his outspoken heroine Beatrice with a marriage to her equal, but he also shows how dangerous silence can be. Hero's silence in the face of the public slander is taken by her father as evidence against her. He says that 'all the grace that she hath left, / Is that she will not add to her damnation / A sin of perjury, she not denies it' (4.1.164–6).

The public slander of Hero demonstrates the value society placed on women's chastity. However, Shakespeare also includes views that are more forgiving. The Friar does not condemn Hero, and believes in her innocence. He also hopes that his plan, of Hero being thought dead, will soften Claudio's attitude such that he would 'wish he had not so accusèd her: / No, though he thought his accusation true' (4.1.225–6). Furthermore, the play presents another character, Margaret, who has been 'unchaste', according to the standards of the day, yet she is not punished. Leonato seems to take a liberal attitude towards her actions.

Thus, in these various ways, Shakespeare's play presents challenges to the idea that women were to be chaste, silent and obedient. Although in the early modern period women were often assumed to be more likely than men to be deceptive and unfaithful, Balthasar's song claims that it is *men* who 'were deceivers ever' (2.3.54).

Interpretation 2: *Much Ado About Nothing* affirms assumptions about women.

Much Ado About Nothing explores the vulnerability of women and ultimately affirms their construction as property. Although Beatrice is initially against marriage, she is eventually tricked into marriage with Benedick. Stephen Greenblatt aptly describes this as a 'benevolent luring' of the quarrelling pair into declarations of love (Greenblatt et al. 2016, p.1395). Although Beatrice is outspoken at the beginning of the play, her marriage to Benedick will result in her losing her independence and becoming Benedick's property, according to early modern ideas.

Women's reputations were particularly vulnerable; a man's word held more weight and the world of public speech was dominated by men (despite a female monarch, Elizabeth I, reigning for much of Shakespeare's life). If Hero is proved false, disturbingly, Leonato threatens that 'These hands shall tear her' (4.1.184). Hero's fate reflects the construction of women as property. Claudio's slander, and Leonato's confirmation that, if she has been unchaste, he would be violent towards her, reflect the negative attitudes towards women in the period.

Even at the comic resolution, the supposed happy ending is undermined by the construction of Hero as property. Leonato says to Claudio, 'I do give you her' (5.4.54), and Claudio claims her as 'mine' (5.4.55). Claudio's repentance for his wrongful slander does not result in any drastic change in his opinion of women; he still judges according to superficial attributes, such as appearance, as implied by his racist comment that he would still marry the veiled bride to keep his word 'were she an Ethiop' (5.4.38).

Furthermore, the engagement of Benedick and Beatrice is tainted by Claudio and Don Pedro's teasing of Benedick as a future cuckold (5.4.44), implying that Beatrice will be unfaithful, and that Benedick himself will be unfaithful (5.4.109), which has some weight, given that Claudio knows Benedick well. This renders the idea of a comic resolution fragile, with lingering questions over whether either Beatrice or Hero will be happy in their married state. They will remain, like most early modern women, with constrained choices and a general lack of agency. Beatrice's feisty independence shown at the beginning of the play may not survive her marriage, due to societal pressures, and Hero will remain vulnerable to Claudio's suspicions, since he does not appear to have undergone any significant reform.

QUESTIONS & ANSWERS

This section focuses on your own analytical writing on the text, and gives you strategies for producing high-quality responses in your coursework and exam essays.

Essay writing – an overview

An essay on a literary work is a formal and serious piece of writing that presents your point of view on the text, usually in response to a given topic. Your 'point of view' in an essay is your interpretation of the meaning of the text's language, structure, characters, situations and events, supported by detailed analysis of textual evidence.

Analyse – don't summarise

In your essays it is important to avoid simply summarising what happens in a text.

- A **summary** is a description or paraphrase (retelling in different words) of the characters and events. For example: 'Macbeth has a horrifying vision of a dagger dripping with blood before he goes to murder King Duncan.'
- An **analysis** is an explanation of the real meaning or significance that lies 'beneath' the text's words (and images, for a film). For example: 'Macbeth's vision of a bloody dagger shows how deeply uneasy he is about the violent act he is contemplating, and conveys his sense that supernatural forces are impelling him to act.'

A limited amount of summary is sometimes necessary to let your reader know which part of the text you wish to discuss. However, always keep this to a minimum and follow it immediately with your analysis of what this part of the text is really telling us.

Plan your essay

Carefully plan your essay so that you have a clear idea of what you are going to say. The plan ensures that your ideas flow logically, that your argument remains consistent and that you stay on the topic. An essay plan should be a list of **brief dot points** covering no more than half a page.

- Include your central argument or main contention – a concise statement of your overall response to the topic.
- Write down three or four dot points for each paragraph indicating the main idea and evidence/examples from the text. Note that in your essay you will need to *expand* on these points and *analyse* the evidence.

Structure your essay

An essay is a complete, self-contained piece of writing. It has a clear beginning (the introduction), middle (several body paragraphs) and end (the last paragraph or conclusion). It must also have a central argument that runs throughout, linking each paragraph to form a coherent whole. See examples of introductions and conclusions in the 'Analysing a sample topic' and 'Sample answer' sections.

The introduction establishes your overall response to the topic. It includes your main contention and outlines the main evidence you will refer to in the course of the essay. Write your introduction *after* you have done a plan and *before* you write the rest of the essay.

The body paragraphs argue your case – they present evidence from the text and explain how this evidence supports your argument. Each body paragraph needs:

- a strong **topic sentence** (usually the first sentence) that states the main point being made in the paragraph
- **evidence** from the text, including some brief quotations
- **analysis** of the textual evidence, with **explanation** of its significance and how it supports your argument
- **links back to the topic** in one or more statements, usually towards the end of the paragraph.

Connect the body paragraphs so that your discussion flows smoothly. Use some linking words and phrases such as 'similarly' and 'on the other hand', though don't start every paragraph like this. Another strategy is to use a significant word from the last sentence of one paragraph in the first sentence of the next.

Use key terms from the topic – or synonyms for them – throughout, so the relevance of your discussion to the topic is always clear.

The conclusion ties everything together and finishes the essay. It includes strong statements that emphasise your central argument and provide a clear response to the topic.

Avoid simply restating the points made earlier in the essay – this will end on a very flat note and imply that you have run out of ideas and vocabulary. The conclusion should be a logical extension of what you have written, not just a repetition or summary of it. Writing an effective conclusion can be a challenge. Try using these tips:

- Start by linking back to the final sentence of the second-last paragraph – this helps your writing to flow, rather than leaping back to your main contention straight away.
- Use synonyms and expressions with equivalent meanings to vary your vocabulary. This allows you to reinforce your line of argument without being repetitive.
- When planning your essay, think of one or two broad statements or observations about the text's wider meaning. These should be related to the topic and your overall argument. Keep them for the conclusion, since they will give you something 'new' to say but still follow logically from your discussion. The introduction will be focused on the topic, but the conclusion can present a wider view of the text.

Sample essay topics

1. "I would fain know what you have to say." (3.5.23)
   In what ways is language used in *Much Ado About Nothing*?
2. How do the ideas of love and war intersect in the play?
3. How does Shakespeare convey and challenge early modern ideas about women in *Much Ado About Nothing*?
4. What roles do the different kinds of humour play in *Much Ado About Nothing*?
5. 'None of the characters changes or develops in the course of the play.' To what extent do you agree?
6. 'Although *Much Ado About Nothing* is a comedy, it also has dark elements that reveal human flaws.'
   Discuss.
7. "Oh villain! Thou wilt be condemned into everlasting redemption for this." (4.2.47–8)
   What role do Dogberry's malapropisms play in *Much Ado About Nothing*?
8. Rhetoric is the art of persuasion. Examine episodes in the play where one or more characters persuade another to do something, and the rhetorical techniques they use.
9. '*Much Ado About Nothing* ultimately presents a positive view of marriage.' Do you agree?
10. 'The two pairs of lovers, Beatrice and Benedick, and Hero and Claudio, are very different, yet there are also similarities.' Discuss.

Useful vocabulary for writing on *Much Ado About Nothing*

Act: a major division in a play. There are five acts in *Much Ado About Nothing*.

Blank verse: plain verse with no rhyming words at the end of the lines.

Dramatic irony: when the audience knows something of which a character is unaware.

Early modern: the early modern period is generally considered to be 1500 to 1800.

Elizabethan: the period in which Elizabeth I was on the throne (1558–1603). Plays written after her death in 1603, when James I became King, fall into the Jacobean period.

Foreshadowing: an idea, event or imagery within a literary or dramatic work that anticipates and indicates an event that will occur later in the narrative.

Iambic pentameter: the rhythmic pattern of a line of verse in which the stresses (beats) fall on every second syllable (iambic), and there are five stresses to a line (pentameter), totalling ten syllables.

Malapropism: an incorrect word that sounds similar to the word intended.

Metaphor: a word or phrase used to describe something else by way of direct comparison.

Oxymoron: a figure of speech in which contradictory terms are used in conjunction.

Personification: a figure of speech in which an abstract idea, inanimate object or animal is given human characteristics.

Prose: speech or written language appearing like ordinary sentences in conversation, without regular rhythm. The word comes from the Latin word *prosa* meaning 'straightforward discourse'. You will recognise it in the play when the sentences run to the edge of the page.

Renaissance: in relation to English literature, the period from the late 1400s until 1660. Shakespeare was writing in the English Renaissance period.

Rhyming couplet: two lines of verse, the last words of which rhyme.

Scene: a subdivision of an act in a play. It also describes the visual appearance of the space in which the action is located.

Simile: similar to a metaphor but using the words 'as' or 'like'.

Soliloquy: a dramatic speech by a single character, usually alone on stage.

Sonnet: poem comprising fourteen lines with a specific rhyming pattern.

Verse: a line of metrical writing. The word 'meter' comes from the Greek word for 'measure' and refers to a pattern of stressed and unstressed syllables. You can often identify it in the play when a character's lines don't continue to the edge of the page. In Shakespeare's plays the verse is mostly in iambic pentameter. (The word 'verse' can also refer to a stanza, which is a paragraph in a poem, and to poetry in general.)

Sample analysis of a topic

'The two pairs of lovers, Beatrice and Benedick, and Hero and Claudio, are very different, yet there are also similarities.' Discuss.

When you first approach an essay topic, the initial step is to think carefully about what the topic is asking you to do. Make sure that you understand all the terms in the topic; if you don't, use a dictionary. Start with some brainstorming using pen and paper, rather than a computer. Put down all your ideas without worrying about how polished they are. Re-read the play carefully and identify some quotations that may be useful for your discussion.

The next step is to draft the essay outline, thinking about how you will structure your essay. The most difficult step is often the framing of your argument. Try to write a draft statement of your main contention at the outline stage. Once you have finished your first draft of the essay you can refine this statement, but it is useful to have a starting position for your argument.

The topic above is asking you to compare and contrast the two pairs of lovers. There are different ways you could approach this. The first body paragraph could focus on one couple's traits, the next paragraph could discuss the second couple's, and then the third paragraph could compare and contrast their characteristics. Alternatively, you could choose themes, such as language and deceptive appearances (as the sample below does), and consider each couple in relation to that theme, before coming to a conclusion at the end of the essay.

Sample introduction

> *Much Ado About Nothing* is one of Shakespeare's most popular comedies, and features two very different pairs of lovers: Benedick and Beatrice, and Claudio and Hero. Both pairs undergo challenges in their relationships before finally joining in marriage; however, the narrative arcs of their journeys throughout the play differ significantly. This essay will compare and contrast the two pairs of lovers, considering the themes of language, and appearance versus reality. Although the two pairs of lovers contrast strongly, they both demonstrate the need to look beyond surface appearances to find deeper truths.

Body paragraph outline

Body paragraph 1

Topic sentence: Language is a key theme of the play and defines the two couples' relationships.

- Start with some general comments about how language and skills in verbal wit were seen as essential to courtly behaviour in Shakespeare's period (providing some historical context to the importance of language in the play).
- Find examples and representative quotations that demonstrate how insults and verbal sparring define the relationship of Benedick and Beatrice in the first half of the play.
- Compare this to Claudio and Hero and their comparative lack of communication, and the consequences of this. You may also wish to consider the paradox that Beatrice and Benedick, with their language skills, initially cause each other pain, whereas Claudio and Hero, by saying almost nothing to each other, become happily engaged.

- Also consider further developments in the play, such as the ways in which language, particularly through poetry, persuades and reveals Beatrice and Benedick to be in love.
- You might also consider how Claudio, in rejecting Hero, uses language in violent ways to construct Hero as damaged property.

Body paragraph 2

Topic sentence: Also relevant to the couples' relationships is the difference between appearances and reality.

- Analyse how Claudio misinterprets surface appearances in rejecting Hero. Consider aspects of Claudio's character traits in this regard, for example the foreshadowing of trouble ahead when Claudio misreads Don Pedro's intentions in wooing Hero.
- Discuss how Benedick and Beatrice appear to hate each other in the early stages of the play; look closely at their speeches for evidence that foreshadows their subsequent change of heart.
- Conclude the paragraph with some observations on how both couples are challenged by appearances and what the consequences of this are.
- Make sure your paragraph includes quotations to support your points.

Body paragraph 3

Topic sentence: Both couples' relationships undergo significant shifts throughout the play.

- Look at key points in the narrative and events that precipitate change for the couples. For example, draw from the scenes where Beatrice and Benedick overhear the staged conversations of their friends, and consider their reflections after hearing these.
- Consider how Claudio has to come to terms with the consequences of his allegations against Hero; how does his attitude change?
- Make some observations about the dramatic effects of these key shifts in the couples' relationships; note any similarities (to help link to the next paragraph).

Body paragraph 4

Topic sentence: At first, the main couples appear to be very different, but there are several key similarities.

- In this paragraph you need to bring your argument back to what the topic is asking you, to think about similarities and differences between the pairs.
- Outline how the couples are quite different; for example, whereas Benedick and Beatrice are loquacious (talk a lot), Claudio and Hero are striking in their lack of communication. What other differences can you think of?
- Next, think about how they are similar. In both couples, partners misread each other and have to learn to adjust their thinking. This idea will then link to your concluding paragraph.

Sample conclusion

> In *Much Ado About Nothing*, the two pairs of lovers at first appear to be strikingly different. Beatrice and Benedick are quick and witty with their language, and their conversations resemble military skirmishes. By contrast, Claudio and Hero are marked by their lack of communication, even when occasion calls for it. Whereas Beatrice and Benedick begin in hate and end in love, Claudio and Hero's initial happiness is ruined as a result of Claudio's unfounded accusations of infidelity. This leads to potential tragedy, before Claudio's repentance and agreement to marry a mystery bride result in the restoration of Hero. What is common to both couples is their initial tendency to misread appearances. The lovers undertake challenging journeys before being rewarded with love, consistent with the comedic genre. Shakespeare's valuable lesson conveyed by the play is not to rely on appearances when the truth is often more complex.

SAMPLE ANSWER

"I would fain know what you have to say." (3.5.23)

In what ways is language used in *Much Ado About Nothing*?

In *Much Ado About Nothing* (1598), language is central to key aspects of the play, such as its themes, plot and sources of humour. This essay will explore three aspects of Shakespeare's language: how it can be used as a weapon, how the misuse of language is a source of humour, and how verse is used to signify rank and to convey emotions. Through these three aspects, Shakespeare illustrates how language is at the core of human experience.

In the play, language is a double-edged sword. The clever use of language is a crucial skill for the upper-class characters, used for display and as a source of enjoyment in exchanging witty insults and observations, as Beatrice and Benedick constantly do. Beatrice cuts Benedick with 'I wonder that you will still be talking, Signor Benedick, nobody marks you' (1.1.86–7). He retorts by calling her 'Lady Disdain' (1.1.88). They both know that words can wound like weapons. The most dangerous insult in the play is Claudio's slander of Hero, orchestrated by Don John. Its destructive power ruins the first wedding ceremony, poisons Hero's public reputation and leads to a kind of 'death' for Hero. She faints and appears dead; moreover, her father at first wishes her dead rather than unchaste, exclaiming 'Do not live, Hero' (4.1.116). The Friar's strategy, of having the family pretend that Hero has 'died' from the slander, is accepted as plausible by the Messina community. Even when she is reconciled to Claudio at the second wedding ceremony, she frames her transformation in terms of the death of the slandered Hero, her previous identity, compared to the newly living exonerated Hero. The slander of Hero has an analogue at the lower level of characters, in that of Dogberry as 'an ass' (4.2.60), an insult that he unwittingly makes worse by repeating, due to his misuse of language.

Such miscommunication and inaccurate use of language is a key source of humour in the play. Dogberry, along with his fellow constable Verges, is particularly characterised by his malapropisms. For example, in the examination scene he says 'opinioned' (4.2.56) instead of pinioned (bound) and 'suspect' (4.2.61) instead of respect. The incorrect words are comical to the audience since they are usually the opposite of what Dogberry intends. What is striking is that often the incorrect word resonates with what is occurring in the play. For example, when Dogberry says 'dissembly' (4.2.1), instead of assembly, this reflects what the watch has inadvertently discovered – the dissembling, or deception, organised by Don John and Borachio. Dogberry's inability to use language correctly leads to miscommunication. Leonato, in frustration, says 'I would fain know what you have to say' (3.5.23). Dogberry's mishandling of language is also a marker of his social rank.

Shakespeare often uses language to signify the different social ranks of characters. Early modern society was hierarchical, and distinctions in social class were conveyed in a variety of ways, from clothing to manners of address. In the plays, verse is generally used by the upper-class characters, prose by the lower. However, upper-class characters may shift to prose to create a particular effect. For example, Claudio and Don Pedro switch to prose in Act 5 Scene 1 (from 5.1.110) to convey how they have been 'lowered' by their actions towards Hero. It is only after they realise their mistake, and their attitude changes to remorse (from 5.1.215), that they revert to verse again. Verse is also associated with love and it is Benedick and Beatrice's attempts to write poetry that betray their true feelings for each other. Even though Benedick struggles to meet the challenge of a sonnet – 'No, I was not born under a rhyming planet, nor I cannot woo in festival terms' (5.2.30–1) – his attempt at 'a halting sonnet' (5.4.87), along with Beatrice's own (5.4.89–90), prove their love and secure the union. As Benedick says, 'A miracle, here's our own hands against our hearts' (5.4.91).

To conclude, the power of language is evidenced throughout the play. It can divide but also bring characters together. Language governs and defines human relationships. Beatrice and Benedick's courtship is characterised by a 'merry war' (1.1.45–6) and, as Benedick observes, they will never be able to 'woo peaceably' (5.2.54). Yet their skills with words are evidence of their lively minds that will keep their marriage alive. Despite Dogberry's mistaken use of words, he and his companions manage to uncover the slander plot and thus undo the damage that threatens Claudio and Hero's marriage. Furthermore, in the final scene, it is the power of poetry that brings Benedick and Beatrice together. Shakespeare thus shows how language is central to human experience, bringing joy, causing pain and conveying our deepest emotions.

REFERENCES & READING

Text

Partington, A & Spencer, R (eds) 2014, *Much Ado About Nothing*, 3rd edn, Cambridge School Shakespeare series, Cambridge University Press, Cambridge.

All quotations and most of the glossary have been drawn from this edition.

References

Ackroyd, P 2005, *Shakespeare: The Biography*, Vintage, London.

Bate, J 1997, *The Genius of Shakespeare*, Picador, London.

——2008, *Soul of the Age*, Penguin, London.

Cartmell, D & Smith, PJ (eds) 2018, *Much Ado About Nothing: A Critical Reader*, Bloomsbury, London.

Cassal, S 2006, 'Shakespeare's Much Ado About Nothing', *The Explicator*, vol. 64, no. 3, pp.139–41.

Daalder, J 2004, 'The "Pre-History" of Beatrice and Benedick', *English Studies*, vol. 85, no. 6, pp.520–7.

De Grazia, M & Wells, S (eds) 2001, *The Cambridge Companion to Shakespeare*, Cambridge University Press, Cambridge.

Dobson, M et al. (eds) 2015, *The Oxford Companion to Shakespeare*, 2nd edn, Oxford University Press, Oxford.

Driver, E et al. (eds) 2009, *The Shakespeare Encyclopedia*, Global Book Publishing, Sydney.

Garber, M 2004, *Shakespeare After All*, Anchor Books, New York.

Gay, P 2008, *The Cambridge Introduction to Shakespeare's Comedies*, Cambridge University Press, Cambridge.

Greenblatt, S 2004, *Will in the World: How Shakespeare Became Shakespeare*, Pimlico, London.

Greenblatt, S et al. (eds) 2016, *The Norton Shakespeare*, 3rd edn, WW Norton & Company, New York.

Kamaralli, A 2018, *Much Ado About Nothing*, Arden Performance Editions, Bloomsbury, London.

Kermode, F 2001, *Shakespeare's Language*, Penguin, London.

Lockerd, BC 2011, 'Symbolism of the Senses: Discursive and Intuitive Reason in *Much Ado* and *Lear*', *The Ben Jonson Journal*, vol. 18, no. 2, pp.212–32.

Myhill, N 1999, 'Spectatorship in/of Much Ado About Nothing', *Studies in English Literature 1500–1900*, vol. 39, no. 2, pp.291–311.

Films

Much Ado About Nothing 1984, dir. Stuart Burge. Starring Lee Montague, Tim Faulkner and Cherie Lunghi.

Much Ado About Nothing 1993, dir. Kenneth Branagh. Starring Emma Thompson, Kenneth Branagh, Denzel Washington, Richard Briers, Keanu Reeves, Robert Sean Leonard and Kate Beckinsale.

Much Ado About Nothing 2012, dir. Joss Whedon. Starring Alexis Denisof, Amy Acker and Fran Kranz.

Websites

British Library, *Much Ado About Nothing*, https://www.bl.uk/works/much-ado-about-nothing

Folger Shakespeare Library 2019, *Much Ado About Nothing*, https://www.folger.edu/much-ado-about-nothing

Minton, G & Werier, C 2019, *Much Ado About Nothing*, Internet Shakespeare Editions, http://internetshakespeare.uvic.ca/Library/Texts/Ado/

Shakespeare Birthplace Trust 2019, https://www.shakespeare.org.uk/